A WORLD IN COMMON
an actor's diary

An intimate look at Richard Nelson's Rhinebeck Panorama

by Jay O. Sanders

Copyright © 2018 Jay O. Sanders.

All rights reserved. No part of this publication may be reproduced, distributed, or transmitted in any for or by any means, including photocopying, recording, or other electronic or mechanical methods, without the prior writted permission of the publisher, except in the case of brief quotations embodied in critical reviews and certain other noncommercial uses permitted by copyright law. For permission requests, write to the publisher at the address below.

ISBN: 978-0-578-41541-3 (Hardcover)
ISBN: 978-0-578-41531-4 (Softcover)
ISBN: 978-0-578-41532-1 (Ebook)

Book design by R. Elizabeth Sanders.

Printed by IngramSpark, in the United States of America.

First printing edition 2018.

Plunder Publishing
92 Lexington Ave., Suite 1100
New York, NY 10016

Front cover: Hong Kong Cultural Center photo: Meg Gibson

Back cover (left to right): Rebecca Sherman, Lynn Hawley, Will Pickens, Amy Warren, Jared Oberholtzer, Shelley Vance, Meg Gibson, Maryann Plunkett, Jay O. Sanders, Richard Nelson, Theresa Flanagan, Mr. So, Roberta Maxwell, Laura Brauner   photo: Jeff Harris

For Richard

JAY O. SANDERS is an American actor/writer who has collaborated with Richard Nelson eight times in the last eight years, experimenting with a bold new form of live theater which explores a simpler overheard experience in place of the traditional presented style. For more than forty years, he has worked extensively in all forms of media, with a special passion for Shakespeare and new plays. In 2015, his own play, *Unexplored Interior*, set in and around the 1994 genocide in Rwanda, was the inaugural production of Washington, D.C.'s Mosaic Theater.

All seven plays which make up the Rhinebeck Panorama so far—the four Apple Family Plays and the Gabriel Family Trilogy—have been filmed by WNET. The Apple plays are archived there but not presently available for viewing, however all three Gabriel plays—*Hungry*, *What Did You Expect?* and *Women of a Certain Age*—can be watched from any computer simply by subscribing to BroadwayHD.com. Our New York production of *Uncle Vanya*, the first-ever production of Gregory Mosher's Hunter Theater Project (a co-production with San Diego's Old Globe Theater), was also filmed by WNET in November, 2018 for *Theater Close-Up*.

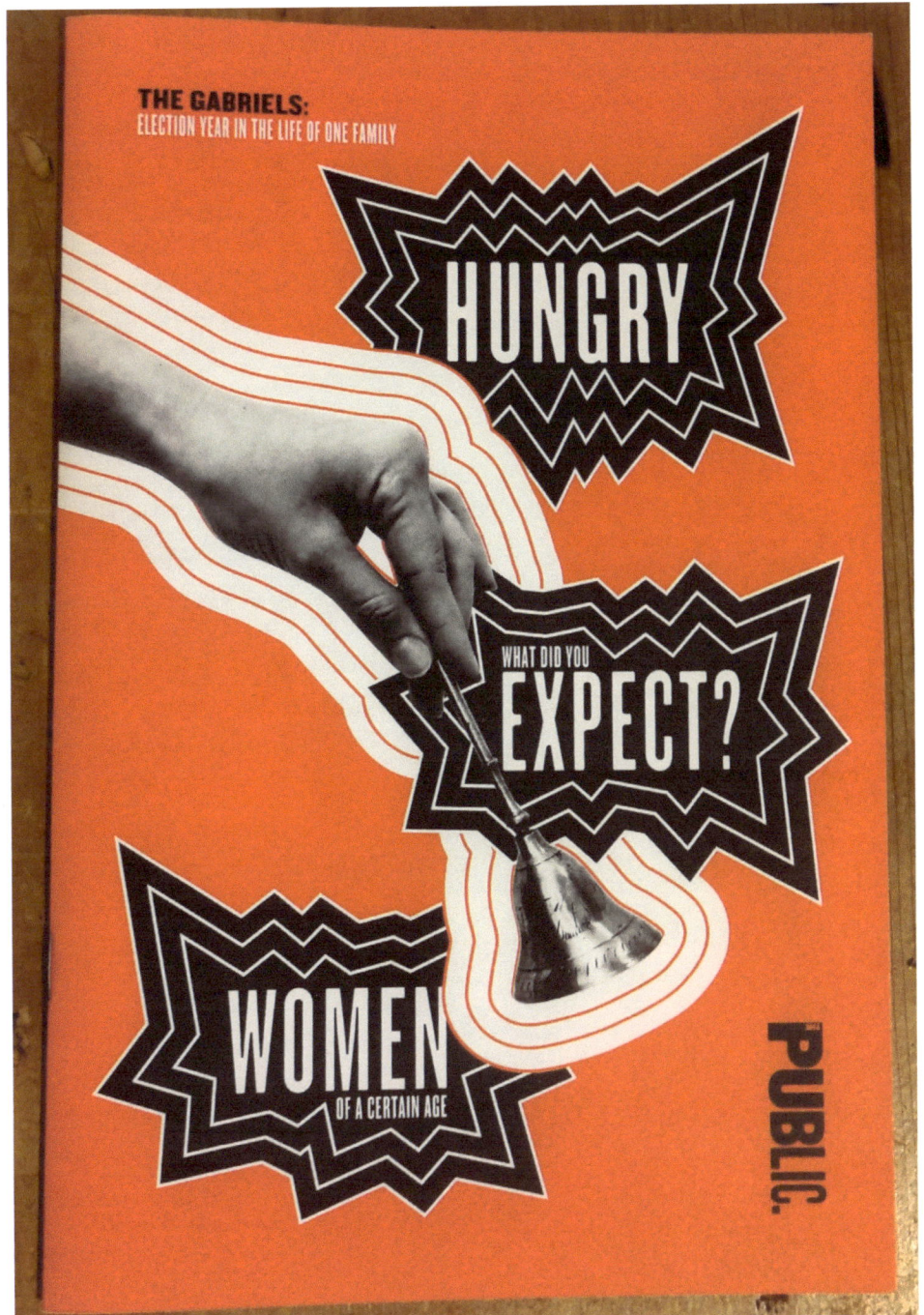

Preface

by Oskar Eustis
Artistic Director, The Public Theater

RICHARD NELSON spent much of the last decade writing two extraordinary cycles of plays about Rhinebeck, New York. They are a great dramatic achievement, and one of the defining monuments of the last decade at the Public Theater. What began as disposable plays, plays Richard assumed would be only for the moment, grew into a detailed, granular psychic portrait of America in the Obama years. I believe they will continue to interest American audiences, artists and scholars far into the future.

What I didn't anticipate was the intense interest in these plays from abroad. In a time when the face America turned to the world was either brutal and military or crude and economic, there was a hunger to hear Americans talk softly to each other with love, anxiety and grace. The international tours of the Apples and the Gabriels were gorgeous models of people to people contact across borders.

For the creation of these cycles, it was necessary that Richard create two acting companies that could stay together and work as an ensemble over an extended period. Both companies were brilliant: Maryann Plunkett and Jay O. Sanders were at the center of both.

What Jay has written here is a rare and precious account of these plays encountering the world. Jay is a gifted writer in his own right, and this Actor's eye description of these journeys is gorgeous and illuminating. It is unusual to see new plays coming to life through the eyes of actors, and the riches of this book are not limited to the Rhinebeck plays. Jay and his wife Maryann are deeply committed artists, who have devoted their lives to the non-profit theater. We have all been blessed by their acting. In these pages, Jay blesses us with his insight.

FIguring out the space with Claire M. Kavanah (Props Designer), Sash Bischoff (Assistant Director), and Richard Nelson

photo: Jason Ardizzone-West

LuEsther Hall at New York City's Public Theater, home to the Gabriels for all of 2016

photo: Jeff Harris

Programs from The Gabriels World Tour, January–June, 2017

Introduction

IN 2015, during a five-week European Tour of Richard Nelson's Apple Plays, I wrote a series of Facebook posts (one for each venue) as an easy way to share that momentous experience with our widely-dispersed friends. Then, in 2016, as we were preparing for our first marathon performances of the Gabriel Trilogy at the Public, Richard said he'd heard about these posts and would love to see them. So, I found all four and emailed them to him. Soon after, he got back to me asking if I'd be interested in doing something similar for our upcoming world tour of the Gabriels.

The difficulty, of course, once the door is open, is knowing how much ground to cover. Richard and I have many shared years of experience in the theater and in life. How much of that should I make use of? My step-by-step choice to devote seven years to these two successive projects, the longest professional commitment of my life, was made easier by the fact that one of Richard's favorite actors, Maryann Plunkett, was also on board. She also happens to be my favorite collaborator…and the woman to whom I've been married for the last 26 years.

So, I eagerly agreed to undertake this task—as a personal expression of our extraordinary experiment and experience, between 2010 and 2017. Hopefully I can offer some useful insights along the way; a window into our process.

Jay O. Sanders at the Brighton railway station — photo: Maryann Plunkett

Author's Foreword

I started acting when I was ten years old, at a very singular, racially integrated community arts center in Cleveland, Ohio, founded in 1917, called Karamu House. It was 1963—right in the heart of our country's impassioned Civil Rights movement and JFK was in the White House—and my father had just been chosen to replace Karamu's founders, who were retiring after forty years there. Located in a predominantly black neighborhood, it was an excitingly unique place. I sang in a youth choir, took drawing classes, and immersed myself in ceramic sculpture. My first acting teacher, Ethel Ballard, was a smart, charismatic, African-American actress who was married to Karamu's technical director, Doc Ballard. The company of actors who performed in the shows were all local, and all had day jobs because they were paid no salary to act. Yet every night, they poured their souls out on Karamu's stages—one proscenium, one arena—performing a wide range of work, including the development and premieres of new plays (many of Langston Hughes' plays were born on these stages), and numerous black and interracial versions of traditionally all-white shows, (i.e. *Guys & Dolls*, *Oklahoma*, *The Music Man*, *The Fantasticks*, *All The Way Home*, and *A Christmas Carol*) a practice unheard of in the U.S. at that time. These actors were my role models, my heroes.

In 1966, my father took a job as director of the teacher-training program with the Peace Corps in Bogotá, Colombia, so our family moved there for two years. When we returned to this country in 1968, Dad began work as Executive Director of the Westchester Council for the Arts, which brought us to Chappaqua, New York—close enough to allow me to begin an important relationship with the New York theater. After a very active relationship with my high school drama department and a gap year working and travelling around South America and Antarctica (a whole other story), I was accepted into the inaugural class of the brand-new theater department at the State University of New York at Purchase, now known as a top training school for actors.

In 1976, when I first entered the professional theater world, there was a vibrant American non-profit theater movement including a large number of very active regional theaters, many of which kept resident companies. They were artistic homes for growth and experimentation, regularly revisiting world classics and exploring new work and finding new voices. Inspired by Peter Brook, Ingmar Bergman, Peter Stein, the Moscow Art Theater, Great Britain's National Theater, Royal Court, and the Royal Shakespeare Company, I yearned to be a part of something extraordinary, something pure and new and without limits. I wanted to be a part of creating a new American Theater.

Fresh out of Purchase, I was cast in speaking roles in both shows of the summer season at my favorite New York venue: Shakespeare-in-the-Park at the Delacorte Theater in Central Park (*Henry V* directed by Joe Papp, himself, and *Measure for Measure*). That Fall, I also was invited to join the company at the Arena Stage in Washington D.C., the most politically-engaged of all the regional theaters, under the direction of co-founder Zelda Fichandler, often called 'the mother of the regional theater movement.' I was contracted for both the season and a State Department-sponsored tour to Czechoslovakia with Arthur Miller's *Death of a Salesman* and David Rabe's *Streamers*, but the tour was cancelled when someone in the government decided that these two plays presented 'too negative a view of the United States.'

In the resulting shuffle, I found myself cast in Arena's new-play series in a strange new one-man piece titled *Scooping*. In it, I played a journalist fed up with simply reporting the news, being an intermediary—I needed to find my own story. In a large, rattan peacock chair, amidst potted palms, I set about interviewing myself, driven to get beyond the stories I'd covered…in search of my own. But the deeper I got, I simply relived more and more violent memories of the stories I'd reported… not mine. So, I take a breath, then start the interview over again, and the lights fade, as I double down on this hopeless, ego-driven cycle.

This wild experiment of a play was made even more so because the entire thing was written using only phrases—one, two, or three words at a time—in restless fits and starts. I was fascinated by the fearless young mind that had conceived and created this unorthodox play. It was the beginning of a lifelong friendship and continuing conversation about the form, necessity, and potential of the theater. That exciting young voice belonged to Richard Nelson.

Richard Nelson's *Scooping* at Washington, D.C.'s Arena Stage, 1977

Thirty-five years later, having maintained our friendship, staying in touch, seeing each other's work, and sharing many of life's passages, Richard and I finally found our way back to work together. He asked me to do the first reading of another experimental new play he had written called **That Hopey Changey Thing** about a reunion of adult siblings from a family called the Apples, set in Richard's own town of Rhinebeck, New York.

Jay O. Sanders

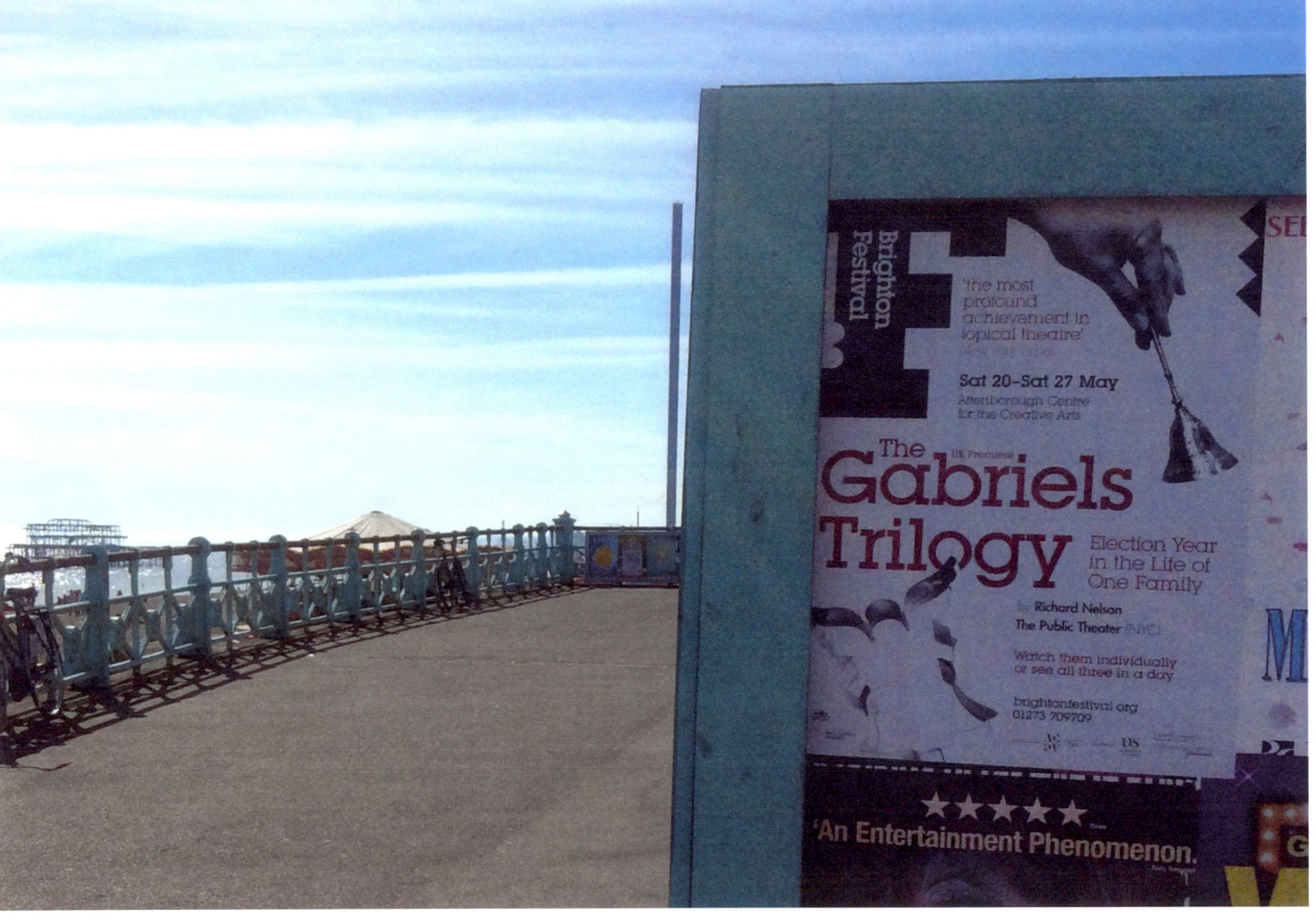

A WORLD IN COMMON

an actor's diary

An intimate look at Richard Nelson's Rhinebeck Panorama

by Jay O. Sanders

With what began as an experiment, a deeply-considered hunch, an instinct borne of a lifetime of work as an extraordinarily prolific American playwright, Richard Nelson has succeeded in reinventing live theater. Pursuing his vision of a form which would speak more simply, more directly, more truthfully to a modern audience which has become inundated with screens and overwhelmed by political noise, he peeled away the artifice. In the Rhinebeck plays, he writes dialogue reflecting the way the people around him really talk, the jagged overlaps and unfinished thoughts of everyday conversation, rather than theatrically heightened speeches. He wanted it to be spoken in the same conversational tones we all recognize from life, rather than the theatrical convention of trained voices lifted to fill a given theater space. So, Richard worked with longtime collaborator and friend sound designer, Scott Lehrer, to find a solution which would allow for a conducive environment in which playing at this level would be possible. No presentation. No theatrical flourish. No unnatural angling of our bodies or faces to 'stay open.' No artifice. The audience is invited to come find us, join us, to gradually come to know the characters who inhabit this world, their relationships, the lives. The goal: to be simply overheard.

Leaning forward as though watching, undetected, through the kitchen window, the audience observes us in our perceived privacy; how we act when we're in a safe place. We live out these bits of our lives with the audience seated around us on three sides, often getting a particular actor's back for a period of time. Characters talk over and interrupt each other, saying things as recognizably banal as conversations often are, peppered and interwoven with the details of daily life. Very little plot, per se, just people unselfconsciously trying to formulate their understanding of who they are, why they find themselves where they are, and looking, like the rest of us, for how to make their way forward. The basic, unifying questions which make us human.

Sometimes, the conversation turns to politics—mostly through genuine questions, confessed confusion, or shared stories of overheard ideas and musings of others, as we try to piece things together; searching. The specifics of the politics of the moment are much less important than the need to talk to others living in the same world, to truly share and be in the company of people we trust, as we attempt to find and maintain our equilibrium in an ever-shifting world.

In 2015, when we toured with the four Apple Family plays to Europe, they resonated loud and clear everywhere we went. Audiences there saw themselves in us which they particularly appreciated because, as we heard repeatedly, it was not the normal image of Americans presented across the world. We came together in recognition that despite life's challenges, its disappointments, changes, and inevitable losses, we all continue to move bravely ahead. We go on.

Setting the Table

FOR BOTH the Apples and our subsequent series, the Gabriels, every performance begins with a ritual which Richard has developed over time. The actors, not yet the characters, one by one enter the space as music plays and set up the room, carefully placing chairs, props, and food across the empty set, making way for life to spill out across the stage and the play to begin. It is a simple, unguarded introduction of actors into the playing space in front of the live audience. An opening of the door. A welcoming in. Together, we will begin to reflect on our lives in this moment in time in a familiar home setting, surrounded by smells of baking bread and freshly chopped onions in place of incense.

photo: Jared Oberholtzer

The Gabriels: Election Year in the Life of One Family

February–December, 2017

Page from Hong Kong Festival Brochure, February, 2017

WE OPENED each of our three plays on the night it actually takes place, so the scripts were written into the future and not officially locked until 4:30 pm the afternoon of the opening, allowing for fresh details and impressions to be woven into the text. The Apples were the same. A line of poetry spoken at the memorial event marking the 50th Anniversary of JFK's assassination, the color of the blazers we had all just seen on tv worn by students singing at the 10-year Commemoration of the 9/11 attacks, the cold dampness of the day, the traffic, the feeling, the life. The Gabriel plays take place on less notable landmarks of our American experience, until the final play, which opened on Election Day, 2016. The other two were spaced out to give an overview of our shared speculative curiosity and reticence—back in March, when the primaries were still going, and in September, after the Conventions had finally yielded the Parties' two candidates. And although the first play, *Hungry*, took place just a day after we had all been assured on national television that the Republican candidate's hand-size should not worry us as to the size of his manhood, no mention is ever made of this, nor even, for that matter, of his name, aside from as a thrown-away blip in a passing tumble of conversation in the very first scene.

For Richard, the landscape that really matters is the family, the house we grew up in, and our immediate surroundings. Everything else is simply the noise beyond, which affects us, of course, but is removed from our more urgent daily needs or reality. Here, in Patricia's kitchen—the family matriarch, now residing full-time at her 'inn,' an independent-living community just a five-minute drive away to which she has recently moved herself—we huddle together to talk, reflect on our recently deceased older brother (whose ashes we have just returned from scattering in the Hudson), and wonder aloud about who we are, how we got here, and where we go from here. All informed by a complicated, human mix of our need to talk, to be known to each other, and share our endless, unanswered questions.

A family of Northeast liberal Democrats; well-educated, artistic, and hard-working, yet feeling the dire economic difficulties of keeping our heads above water, the fast-changing world presses in hard on all sides. We reason, we joke, we prod, and ask familiar questions like *'Whatever happened to interest from a bank?'* Like most of the country, guided by endless poll numbers and talking heads, we all believe that Hillary Clinton is soon to be our first woman president, but we even worry about that. *'What will come of all the rhetoric? How will it translate into what really affects our lives? What about us?'*

The quest to create a new form of theater that can bridge the divide between us and our audience is a daring and important one. Peter Brook explored the simple power inherent in 'the empty space' which would invite our imaginations to fill in the gaps and details around the drama, a co-conspiracy of artists and audience to help us to delve deeper into the world of the play. Imagination unadorned, unhidden, vulnerable. Richard has been looking for his own way to carve out that place in live theater, to refine what we do to connect freshly in a time when the audience has spent hours and hours watching close-up images of people in the myriad screen forms ubiquitous in our everyday lives. The moment a stage actor enters, turns front, and raises their voice, a distance is created between us and our audience.

What Richard has evolved is a wholly new approach, an overheard observational theater. In the desire to distinguish what we're doing from terms such as *'realism'* or *'naturalism,'* Richard calls it *'verisimilitude.'* We do not pretend to be real—we are actors playing on a minimal set in a theater with an audience present, sitting as close as possible, some even overlapping onto our space. Our acting is not *'naturalism'*—we don't *'um'* and *'ah'* to create the effect of being natural. We simply enter and live on the stage, a working kitchen, and make a meal as we talk and listen to each other.

We started it as an experiment with the Apple Family. A grid of nine highly sensitive microphones was hung over our heads, allowing us to speak in conversational tones, in whatever direction we happened to be facing, offering an unselfconscious setting for our characters to live in and their stories to be revealed. On the way to making it work, we went through a great deal of trial and error, of course, often eliciting complaints of *'why can't they speak louder?'* But the goal was to create a space in which our audience would need to lean forward, to listen and observe as they would in life. The customary practice of actors pushing out a performance to allow the

> **On the way to making it work, we went through a great deal of trial and error, of course, often eliciting complaints of *'why can't they speak louder?'* But the goal was to create a space in which our audience would need to lean forward, to listen and observe as they would in life.**

audience to sit back and be taken for a ride was being challenged. *You must listen differently—engage with your careful attention; you are welcome to come find us.*

Those who got it, were handsomely rewarded with an experience many claimed to have never had before—these characters, these people, the Gabriels (as with the Apples) became familiar to them, extensions of their own family, having conversations about daily life, relationships, and eventually the politics of the moment in a way that wasn't being offered anywhere else. Free of punditry, political partisanship, or argument—just human interaction. Richard's choice was to make the Gabriels a reflection of our New York City, Public Theater audience (which is 99.9 percent Northeastern Liberal Democrats) and allow them to air their deepest questions and confusion about the state of the country in a completely safe home environment (*'Can't I ask that? The doors and windows are closed. No one's listening…'*). The opportunity for the audience to overhear honest doubts and fears spoken by people like themselves was wholly unique. In the first Apple play, for example, rather than take easy jabs at Sarah Palin, we dared to question Obama's choices and qualifications (despite the fact that we had all clearly voted for him). We offered room for honest self-reflection where we wouldn't be judged for asking unpopular questions. (Richard has noted that had he been writing these plays to open in Dallas, the family would have needed to be Republican for the same reason.)

Richard referred to the first of these experiments—**That Hopey Changey Thing**—as *'a disposable play'* because the details and references were all so incredibly specific that he feared they might lose their relevance and interest to audiences removed in time and place. It proved to be quite the opposite—the very specific truth of the moment translated to a universal recognition. Five years later, when we toured the four Apple plays to Germany, England, and Austria, the audiences recognized us as themselves, completely, despite the different

Roberta Maxwell (Patricia Gabriel) making friends in Perth   photo: Maryann Plunkett

street names, local markets, and politicians (a glossary was provided in the program for reference)—none of that mattered. They saw their own lives, their own struggle to make sense of their lives, their own helplessness. In Brighton, we performed a marathon of all four plays for full houses of mostly British liberals who were about to have their own major national elections two days later—one in which their party was predicted to do extremely well, but ended up losing everything. All the tensions they were feeling were embodied onstage in front of them, much the way we feel watching Chekhov's creations (which have always fascinated Richard) in their own detailed settings of life in their very specific time and place, immediately predating the Russian Revolution. But Chekhov didn't have the same technology available to him to help surmount the theatrical convention of raised voices.

Hence, a new form, to reach today's audience in an age of constant screen interaction, was made possible by Richard's vision. His carefully-crafted, observational dialogue sounds eerily unscripted (*'How much of that do you all improvise?'* —None of it.), his insistence on non-theatrical movement and motivation, and his collaboration with sound designers Scott Lehrer and Will Pickens. As we all explored this new territory together, they developed a more and more effective grid of microphones (nine above the Apples, the Gabriels play with 14).

In order to make clear how much thought and detail goes into this aspect of our work, I asked Will to help me make the full task of this unique sound project clear. So, here it is:

Speakers are hung strategically overhead to keep the sound as balanced and even as possible throughout the space. Each microphone is individually delayed to each speaker. This allows the conversational voices to be raised, or augmented for the people who are looking at backs or are farther away but it still feels like the voice is coming from the character speaking, not from the speakers.

The voice is a focused cone of sound. It is directional. When a voice is directed at you, you feel it, like a spotlight. This can be a problem when an audience is listening in to a conversation around a table, which is where much of our plays happen. Wherever you happen to be sitting in the audience, there is always a person looking away from you. The goal of the sound system is to help the audience hear that which is not directed at them. When it works just right, the audience member doesn't even realize the sound system is on. They can just better hear the person speaking. It is never loud, never in your face, it is transparent. There is a cognitive disconnect when we cannot see the actor's lips move. So, we teach the audience to lean forward and listen in on our conversation, removing that learned barrier.

The voice moves in a straight line at the speed of sound. The energy of the voice dissipates as it moves farther from the actor. Because the amount of power of the voice is intentionally low in a production like this. The voice needs to be picked up and augmented for the audience. To maintain the directionality of the voice the signal of the voice must be delayed so that it matches the same line that voice is coming from.

Imagine a person is 40' feet away from you onstage. Their voice will take about 35ms to get to you. If we want to augment that voice we need to pick it up and deliver it to you in about 35ms so that it feels like it is coming from the same location as the actor. If we take a microphone in front of the actor and send it directly to the speaker you would first hear the voice from the speaker and then hear the live voice. So, we want to source to the voice from the actor, not from the

Preparing to fly Will's speaker grid   photo: JOS

loudspeaker. To do this, we delay the sound travelling from microphone to speaker.

If we delay the mic 35ms, then it will arrive a little too late, like a small echo of the live voice. We also need to take into account the distance of the speaker. If you take the distance from the actor to the audience member, subtract the distance from the speaker to the audience member, then multiply that by the speed of sound, we get closer to being inline with the actor's voice.

Understanding that equation, we then multiply it by the number of speakers, and again, by the number of microphones. In the largest configuration that is 24 speakers and 14 microphones, giving us 336 delay points. Once the speakers are delayed properly, then the volumes of the speakers need to be balanced. And when all this is done, a live sound mixer (in this case, the indispensable Laura Brauner) then follows the levels and movements of the actors, mixing the hanging microphones. Extraordinarily sophisticated stuff, all in the service of erasing any awareness of anything being there at all!

The legendary Jennifer Tipton's lighting has also evolved over the seven years we've been at this, playing with the right balance to keep the audience in the room with us while still focusing the eye on the playing area. During the short breaths of shifting time (seconds or minutes gone by) as we physically reposition ourselves to embody the jump forward in time there were quick blackouts coupled with a recorded sound cue resembling a human exhale. In the earlier cycle (the Apple plays), Jennifer would subtly bring lights up on the audience as they faded on us, gently keeping their awareness of themselves in the space. But for the Gabriel plays—in a different space—it seemed to be inappropriate to light the audience during the quick blackouts. There seemed to be enough light on the audience during the scenes, reflected from the stage.

For each play, Jennifer began with the cue (there was always—by chance—only one cue for each whole play) for the last play. This was a coincidence—not planned. The principle was that the light for each scene as well as each play would be the same; that the light would be changed only if the staging situation made it necessary. It turned out to be the same needed for each scene in a play but each play would need different light from the one before and the one after it. The plan for light was fluid and open to change as made necessary by the positions and movement of the cast in each play.

The lighting on tour is ever-changing in its nature. The light must change because of a different auditorium, a different configuration of the audience, differently colored walls or curtains or for any of a myriad reasons. The person recreating the light (in this case, Jeff Harris) has to maintain the sense of place for the cast while making sure that the look is as close to the original as possible for the audience—a constant, new challenge for each new venue.

Laura Brauner (Live Sound Mixer) with fresh loaf of *Hungry* bread
photo: Jared Oberholtzer

Susan Hilferty's scenic design for all the plays has been purposely spare; a few rugs, tables, some mismatched chairs. In the case of the Gabriels, (where she collaborated with Jason Ardizzone-West) adding a desk, a bench, and a refrigerator, stove, and sink—all functional, evoked the seductive familiarity of hanging out in the kitchen, deepened by the actual smells of fresh food being prepared, bread being kneaded and baked, and the comforting rhythms and sounds of pouring, slicing, dicing, and chopping. Home.

As I described earlier, in the opening moments of each play, the actors engage in a ritual dance of setting the scene to music, adorning bare surfaces with well-worn kitchenware, cookbooks, photos on the fridge, remnants of food, pot-holders, salt and pepper. The magic sweeps in, breathing life into a barren terrain, a swirl of bodies as the nest is feathered, actors to places, the music concludes, lights down, then up, and the play begins.

Susan also designs our costumes, assisted by Mark Koss and Andrea Hood. She has worked in close collaboration with Richard for many years and countless productions, her choices carefully avoiding comment. She dresses us comfortably, often starting with clothes we wear in our own lives, appropriate to the setting, and the weather of each play's date, but without indicating to the audience who we are. There's plenty of time for the audience to discover our professions, relationships, and various inner workings without descriptive clues telling our stories for us. This way, we all arrive onstage as blank human slates, to be gradually discovered in all our complexity.

Throughout both Rhinebeck series, Richard also engages actor and audience in another conversation, an exploration of the very nature of the Theater itself; the plays and players, the traditions, the lore, the playwrights, even the role of the audience. Having spent a lifetime as a prolific playwright, translator, dramaturg, teacher, and, of course, audience, he offers many long-considered thoughts and observations through various characters and conversations.

> ...we all arrive onstage as blank human slates, to be gradually discovered in all our complexity.

In the Apples, Uncle Benjamin, (brought richly to life by Jon DeVries), was a study of a highly skilled and experienced older actor who had recently suffered a heart attack, causing him to lose a significant amount of his short-term memory. By introducing a younger actor, Jane Apple's boyfriend, Tim, into those plays, someone who knows and reveres Benjamin's talent and history, questions are posed about the nature of who we are as actors if we no longer have our memory. We gradually discover all sorts of treasures still alive in his instincts and craft, and one level of his skills actually heightened by his condition, because Benjamin effortlessly achieves what most actors are constantly in search of—to forget…thereby allowing him to genuinely perform each scene or story for the first time. Having watched Benjamin give a reading performance in New York City of some of Oscar Wilde's writings, the younger actor, Tim, shares the term he and his actor friends have come up with to describe it: *willed amnesia*. Benjamin likes this. A lot.

For the Gabriels, our recently-deceased brother, son, husband, and brother-in-law, Thomas, was a playwright. A rather familiar one. Richard lays himself open, in the same way he asks his actors to, offering up a complex self-portrait—competitive, hopeful, teasing, politically-curious, judgmental, well-read, self-involved, loving, driven, thoughtful, truth seeker…wrestling with his own human contradictions. And with ours.

Women of a Certain Age, the third play of the Gabriel Trilogy, opened on Election Day, November 8, 2016. As with much of the rest of the world, in New York City there was a general assumption that

Hillary Clinton was about to be elected our first woman President. The overwhelmingly positive response to our opening night performance—the birth of this beautiful play, completing the trilogy—turned surreally into one of the great shocks of our time, as the election returns—being broadcast on televisions in the Public Theater lobby as part of our opening night party—silenced us all.

A cloud of sadness and confusion seemed to hang in the air. Our audience's subsequent need to sit with us and listen was palpable, as if they'd all come out in search of community and spiritual triage. The need just to be together with other human beings was tantamount.

In *Women of a Certain Age*, as George Gabriel, I quote Nigerian visual artist El Anatsui who said that through *'our capacity as human beings to create out of our mess…we celebrate being human.'* Artists as celebrants, priests. Thomas' widow Mary says, *'Thomas always said theater and religion* [interconnecting her fingers] *are like this.'* extending back to the earliest, most culturally-imperative theater of the Greeks. We, too, include the power of religious ritual, echoed in our own setting of the scene at the opening of each play. We gather, the space is blessed, and we begin. With every step, we are trying to understand and give meaning to our human condition with better and better metaphors, images, and questions, to see more clearly who and what we are. The opening line of *Women of a Certain Age*—'Who's there?'—is discussed later in the same play as being Thomas' idea of the greatest opening line of all time of any play (*Hamlet*). In his words, *'Every play should begin with that line: 'Who's there?'!'*

Gabriels Tour props roadbox

photo: Theresa Flanagan

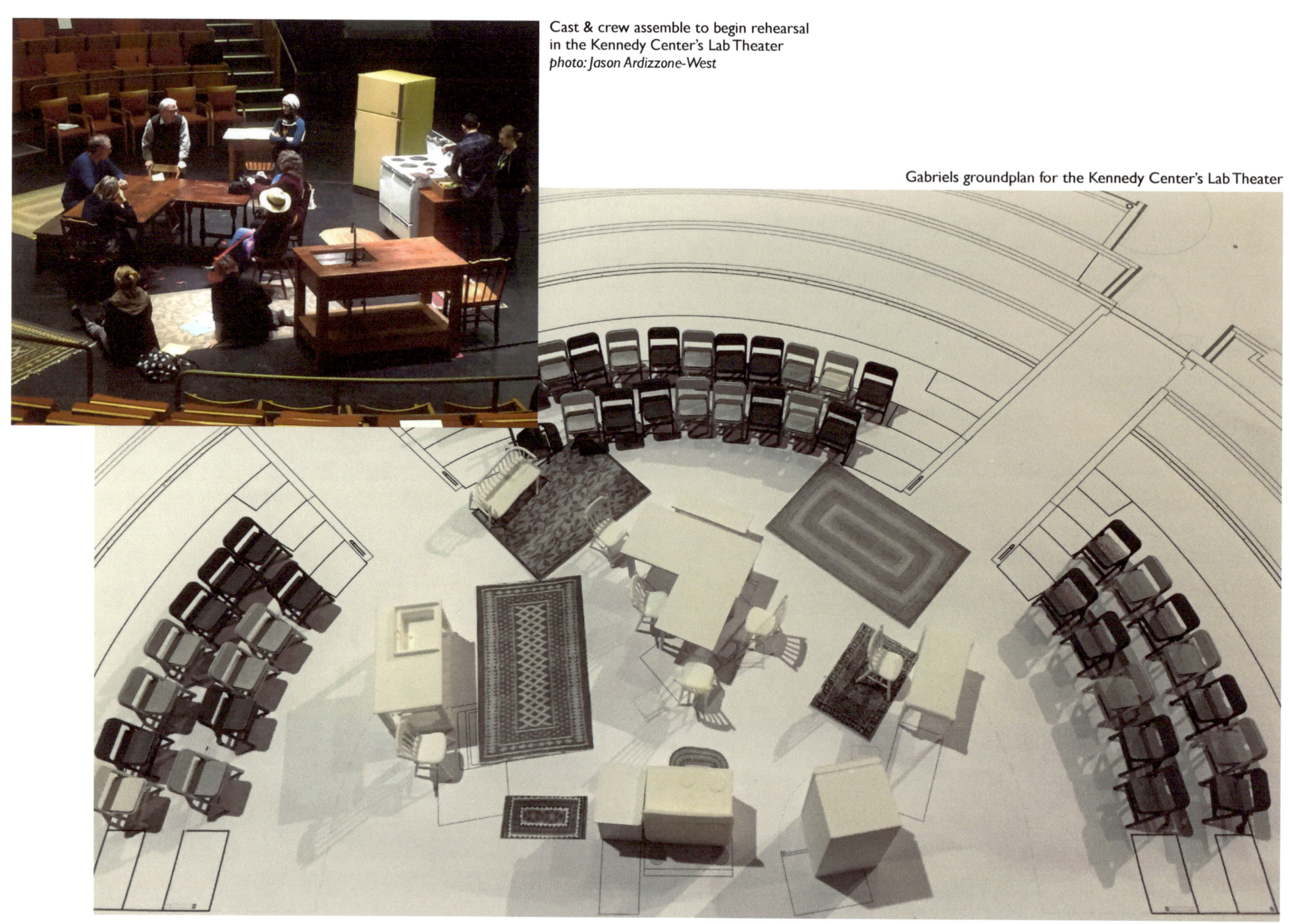

Cast & crew assemble to begin rehearsal in the Kennedy Center's Lab Theater
photo: Jason Ardizzone-West

Gabriels groundplan for the Kennedy Center's Lab Theater

A WORLD IN COMMON *an actor's diary*

The Gabriels On Tour: Washington D.C.

January, 2017

THE KENNEDY Center was built as a living monument to the Arts. Seated majestically on the banks of the Potomac, it exemplifies our country's commitment to the necessity of what artists do. However, aside from a very few exceptions, the Kennedy Center has mostly been a roadhouse for proven commercial productions rather than a supporter of new voices or daring experimental ventures. In the theater we have been booked for our three-week run, the Theater Lab, a crowd-pleasing production of *Shear Madness* has been in residence for the last 25 years. Breaking with this tradition, the newly-appointed producers of this space decided to expand the philosophy of the space, and we were selected to be their first step towards beginning a new conversation with the audiences here.

The space, itself, is warm and wonderfully conducive to the environment we are trying to create. The main difference from our original home in the LuEsther Hall at the Public Theater, is the distance between the front rows and our playing area. At the home in which we gave birth to this venture over the last year, we had audience members seated right up next to us, the legs of some people reaching into our space, overlapping our lives. But in D.C., we have a four- or five-foot buffer zone to contend with, setting us out on our own little island of light, which worried us. Fortunately, the extraordinary sound design and clear sightlines of the audience wrapping around us in the ¾ circular permanent seating of this theater succeed in bridging that gap, maintaining the necessary intimacy of our environment.

The Gabriels Tour begins—*left to right:* Richard Nelson, Lynn Hawley, Maryann Plunkett, Will Pickens, Jared Oberholtzer, Shelly Vance, Jay O. Sanders, Meg Gibso, *kneeling:* Rebecca Sherman & Theresa Flanagan, Laura Brauner, Roberta Maxwell, Amy Warren *photo: Jeff Harris*

Jay O. Sanders

Obviously, these plays are particularly resonant at this moment in our country's history, and to be performing them in the heart of our country's seat of power in the days immediately leading up to and just after the presidential inauguration only heightens their importance as oases of gathering and reflection. But there has been some concern about anticipated audience size, given both the distractions of the ongoing political climate, especially in this town, and the producers' learning curve of how to publicize and sell our three separate weekday shows leading up to the two weekend marathons.

As it turns out, our weekday houses are only half-full, but the focus, engagement, and response of those who are there is profound. We can feel it. We are filling a much-needed role for this community, too. We are necessary theater. As the audiences grow substantially for our weekend marathons, the shows play to the same sense of necessity.

Throughout the life of both the Apples and the Gabriels, one of the most common remarks we hear from audience members is, 'I forgot I was watching a play, I thought I was sitting at the table with you and almost joined in the conversation. I almost said something out loud.' At one of our marathon performances of **Hungry**, when (as George Gabriel) I was trying to remember the name of the billionaire Bill Clinton pardoned during the last days of his Presidency, I said 'That really rich guy— Mark…' and someone sitting down front instinctively answered: 'Rich!' (They were right, of course.) Without missing a beat, Lynn Hawley (playing my wife, Hannah) also said it, as scripted, and on we went,… but we were all smiling inside at just how closely they were listening.

> *Nelson has taken everyday life, ordinary existences, captured them …without spectacle or artifice…so very simple it defies explanation in how moving and extraordinary it becomes.*
> Amanda Gunther—Theatre Bloom

> *We're true eavesdroppers on the Gabriels; Nelson's actors speak in conversational tones that will at times strike some theatergoers as overly hushed. Although a matrix of 14 or so microphones hangs over the stage and something like 20 speakers are suspended above the audience, one does have to strain to catch all of the dialogue…nuances of character and relationship…make even an exchange of glances seem as if it's a twist of the plot…Major storms, even catastrophes, may be brewing in the world, but they like the rest of us, know only how to get by, one small moment at a time.*
> Peter Marks—Washington Post

The day of the inauguration is a day off for us. None of us being supporters of the new President, to put it mildly, we variously find ways to distract ourselves, some venturing out to get a feel of the attending crowds (now made famous by the new President's odd continual assertions about their unsurpassed ranks). Then, the next morning—on the opposite side of the spectrum—a bunch of us assemble at the Kennedy Center to receive the three buses which arrive teeming with friends from the Public Theatre, all to attend the Million Women March. We welcome them with coffee, donuts, and bathrooms before sending them off to participate in what turns into the largest worldwide protest demonstration in history, as we head up for our first marathon of the tour. To say the least, our country is deeply divided and in desperate need of conversation.

all bread photos by Jared Oberholtzer

Signs of Life

THE PROPS used in The Gabriels are a wide array of kitchen tools, foodstuffs, pots and pans, hot pads, cookbooks, magazines, family photographs, notebooks, and other memorabilia that find their way into a long lived-in home. Carefully chosen by our prop master, Claire M. Kavanah, to serve and reflect our lives, they are essential to the heart of these plays. As we travelled, they were painstakingly managed by Shelly Vance, and our stage managers, Tess Flanagan and Jared Oberholtzer, who juggle, set-up, and catalogue of all of these objects and food elements, from apples and avocados to onions, olive oil, garlic, and parsley, across continents and time zones.

In **Hungry**, for example, raw bread dough is prepared for the top of every show. Mary (Maryann Plunkett) takes it out of the refrigerator, kneads it, then puts it into the oven in beginning of the first scene, and every show, an hour later, it comes out perfectly on cue, risen, golden brown, and filling the theater with heavenly smells, to the audible delight of all in attendance. The magic of everyday life, played out in real time right in front of them. Even so, we always have a few

deniers—the *dough-doubters*—who assume these perfect loaves must be produced by sleight-of-hand, some theater trick, despite the overwhelming evidence of their senses.

Our backstage team's work is a show unto itself, and we are all dependent on the loving attention they give to the purchasing, readying, and placement of food, books, and kitchen utensils, keeping track of it all. In Brighton, the props for all three plays are laid out across the stage to take stock of everything we're travelling with, so I thought it important to include that photo here as a key part of the record of our journey.

Monster guards a loaf of fresh bread

Taking stock of three shows worth of props on the set in Brighton   photos: Jared Oberholtzer

Perth, Australia

February 3–23, 2017

I BEGIN THE Far East leg of our tour with a mammoth faux pas…in the form of a passport which had expired a month earlier. Maryann and I arrive in a timely fashion to JFK, where we go directly to check in, and I am confronted with this bombshell which set me off on a wild excursion, racing back to our apartment in the City to locate the correct one and get back to the airport within a 2½ hour window—during rush hour. Fortunately, on my way to the taxi stand, I happen onto a professional limo driver now working solo who brazenly agrees to take on the challenge. He somehow winds us around and through the hectic mess of commuters heading into the City and gets me to the West Village remarkably fast, where I then engage in a desperate search for my up-to-date passport, finally resulting in success (while shocking the hell out of our 22-year-old son, Jamie, who thought I was long gone). We then race back out the other way past the Verrazano Bridge, and somehow make it to the airport by exactly 8:30 am—half an hour to go! Unfortunately, given Cathay Pacific's limited ground crew, they have decided it's too late for me to make it onto the flight, and I am forced to wait for the next one out, a few hours later. So, my adventure begins with a 25-hour flight separate from the rest of the company, including my wife who doesn't get confirmation I am safely on the next flight until they land in Hong Kong 17 hours later to switch flights for the second leg to Perth. When I finally rejoin them in Australia, our body clocks are so confused that time becomes an abstract concept and naps a matter of survival.

Rehearsing in Perth photo: Jeff Harris

On our first day of rehearsal at the Subiaco Arts Centre—our home for the next two weeks—we begin to adjust to a very different space than either the LuEsther at the Public or the Kennedy Center Lab. The stage here sits about a foot above the floor of the front row, and the ceiling overhead is substantially lower. Here we go. We are welcomed by Wendy Martin, Artistic Director of the Perth International Arts Festival (PIAF), who steps up onto the set with us and becomes suddenly overwhelmed with emotion. She had seen the Apples in Vienna on our tour two years ago, then flew over to see **What Did You Expect?** (the middle Gabriel play) at the Public last September. Taking a deep breath, she looked around at all of us and finally spoke. '*I can't believe we finally got you here. What Richard's doing, what you're doing—these plays—it's so important right now. Especially in light of this political atmosphere. We welcome you. We need your conversation. Thank you!*'

Our dear friend, Ruth Sternberg, Production Executive of the Public Theater, arrives for a few days to make sure we are all set to go at the theater and get a quick look around Perth before she has to get back to meetings and problem-solving back home. Around our rehearsals and performances we all explore, in various configurations, the waterfront (walkable from our hotel), Rottnest Island, the extraordinary beaches, and the old town of Fremantle with its various stores and restaurants, Shipwreck Museum, Arts Center (housed in an old insane asylum), and famous Fremantle Prison (Magwitch, the convict character in *Great Expectations*, was said to have escaped from the ship transporting him to Fremantle). We also make our way up the hill to King's Park, the largest city park in the world with spectacular views of the city and water below, to witness the final night of the Perth Festival's remarkable audiovisual installation, *Boorna Waanginy; The Trees Speak*, featuring an impressive show of images projected across the trees, as the story of Perth's birth and evolution played out in music and narration around us. We were told that over 50,000 residents have come through to experience it.

Back in town, the company is invited to attend *Exit/Exist* which turns out to be the perfect opening performance for this multi-cultural festival. The extraordinary South African dancer/choreographer, Gregory Maqoma evokes the feeling of a Greek ritual, starting onstage in modern dress to a soundtrack which combines the hypnotic drone of electronic rhythms with the acoustic tones of live guitarist Guiliano Modarelli. Maqoma's hands begin to vibrate, buzzing with focused energy, which then moves gradually up into his whole body, setting off every imaginable isolation—working his way (and guiding us with him) back in time. Eventually, he is joined by the four-man Vuyani Ensemble, an *a cappella* group (also from South Africa) made up of a striking range of voices which cry out individually one moment then erupt together the next, woven in tight, exotic harmonies which lift us collectively to the heavens and hold us there, suspended. One of the singers puts a hat on Maqoma's head who begins to dance in every direction and variation without ever losing it from his head. This was Richard's favorite part. He saw it as a slave's dance of defiance—you can put your stupid hat on me, but you can't limit me, can't keep me from being who I am. The singers also bring on a bowl of water, two bags of sand, and a large cup of oil—elements which become the sacred tools of our celebrant. Gregory, now stripped down to just a pair of black shorts and an animal-skin garment, portrays the revered Xhosa warrior chief on whom the piece centers. He buries a pair of horns he has danced with in one pile of sand, makes a circle in the center of the stage with the other, offers water and sand to his singers as a sort of communion blessing, and finally pours the oil down his body, gleaming in the lights, as his new glow seems to consecrate him, and us. We all come spontaneously to our feet, everyone in the theater feels it—the Perth International Arts Festival has just clearly—electrically—begun!

In our two weeks in Perth, over the course of eight days, we play five marathons…and once again, the audience response is profoundly personal. They knew us. However, before we start performing, during the dress/tech rehearsal of our three plays, we come offstage from the first play (**Hungry**) to find a seriously flustered Richard, '*You're yelling—too loud! Too loud!!*' I am genuinely confused. '*The show seemed pitched right where we'd been playing it,*' I tell him. '*I had Will turn off all the mics during the show,*' he insists, '*and it was still too loud!*' After some discussion with all of us in the dressing room, we agree it must be the low ceiling and hard back walls. We're also adjusting to extremely different entrances and exits in this space, but that seems to be working out fine. We agree to try bringing it down and trust they can hear us. It doesn't take much, once we begin play two (**What Did You Expect?**) to find our new

Gregory Maqoma in *Exit/Exist*   photo: Suzy Bernstein

Sign from Perth's King's Park celebrating the seasons   photo: JOS

Jay O. Sanders

range—actually, it is a revelation. To be able to speak this intimately, more quietly than we've ever done before—and know it is enough—is enormously freeing. This time, we come offstage to find a beaming, greatly-relieved Richard. *'That's it! Can you feel it?'* he asks. *'You must feel it!'* We all do. Meg Gibson (who plays Karin) says she actually finds it a little scary. Playing at this level, she says, waves of emotion keep flooding through her in a way she's never experienced before. She's never felt so vulnerable onstage. The rest of the run here proves to be a whole new experience of these plays which will inform our understanding and playing of them from here on in. Everything we thought we knew about them is deepening.

The day before our final Australian marathon and the move to Hong Kong, our whole group is invited back to King's Park, where we had experienced the impressive sound-and-light show, for a *Welcome to Country* ritual to be performed by a member of the local indigenous community. Awareness here of this land having been appropriated from its aboriginal inhabitants is very strong. It's even included as part of the opening announcement before each show at the festival—*'Please turn off your cell phone and we remind you that this is all taking place on Nyoongar land,'* regularly honoring Australia's history.

Perth audience diners on the hill outside the theatre between plays   photo: Meg Gibson

Nelson's brilliant work…is one of the most germane pieces of theatre being shown anywhere in the world. It hints presciently at Donald Trump's rise and the shifting sands of sociopolitics in America while simultaneously imparting a touching tale of familial grief with deft sensitivity. The Gabriels is a singularly remarkable piece of theatre, and, for what it's worth, was my pick of the festival…

TM Douglas—The Australian

…how rare it is to see 'women of a certain age' centre stage as well-rounded characters in their own right…The fact that they wear minimal or no make-up is also refreshing…a quiet, compelling masterpiece.

Richard Watts—Arts Hub

This isn't a debate play—the Gabriels barely argue and never raise their voices—but the ideas with which they gently grapple are undeniably political…it becomes clear that there's something epic about the mere act of living through a year with family…you've borne witness to something quite special.

Ben Neutze—Daily Review

Hong Kong trilogy inspired by the Apple Family Plays

Hong Kong, China

February 24–March 5, 2017

MY FIRST impression of this world class business hub is exactly what I'd been told—*NYC on steroids*. Construction everywhere, endless high-rise buildings. One of the most striking details for me is the cross-hatching of construction scaffolds everywhere around us rising high into the air, all made from bamboo. I had been told about this but actually seeing it is one of the most memorable aspects of this city for me. We are staying in Kowloon, and the Hong Kong Cultural Center we're performing at is located only a few blocks from our hotel—the Marco Polo Gateway—along the harbor. Between us and the enormous theater complex stretches one continuous indoor mall of international high-end designer stores, as if Fifth Avenue and Times Square had been put into a blender, then poured out onto the streets, flashing and painting them with *Bladerunner*-like images of young pouting models.

We are invited to a Dim Sum welcome lunch and are introduced to Mr. So, the man who had been taken enough with the Apple plays at the Brighton Festival two years ago, that he commissioned a Chinese playwright he knew to write a trilogy of plays about a Hong Kong family. He also began straightaway to arrange to bring us over to the Hong Kong Arts Festival, and now, two years later, here we are.

The Gateway Hotel has bottomless breakfasts that seem to range on forever—everything, both sweet and savory; big bowls of raspberries and blueberries, muesli, and fresh juices, any form of coffee, custom-made omelets, a wide range of breads and pastries of various national origins, bacon, sausage, eggs, tomato, smoked salmon,

Oskar entertains the troops at *Ozone* in Hong Kong   photo: Maryann Plunkett

onion, Dim Sum, Indian curries, on and on. In Perth, we all had mini-apartments with kitchens and even laundry, so we'd been shopping and making breakfast for ourselves. But this now becomes the standard by which we'll all compare the breakfast buffets at the various hotels along the tour.

Men approach you on the street the way drug dealers do in New York, but here, they're slipping us fliers for tailor shops. This is one of the main cultural advantages known across the world about visiting Hong Kong. Custom suits, dresses, shirts, whatever, artfully constructed for extremely affordable prices in very short order. A quick ride on the Star Ferry takes us across the harbor to more interconnected malls, as well as hillside staircases, alleyways, and moving walkways to outdoor stalls selling colorful masks, wigs, t-shirts, etc. Maryann and I ride the Hong Kong Observation Wheel which lifts us to stunning overviews of the harbor. Eventually, most of us also make our way up to the popular city overlook, Victoria Peak, accessible by a steep cable car ride.

Oskar Eustis, Artistic Director of the Public Theater, and his wife, Laurie, have both flown over to meet up with our tour here. We all get dressed up for a celebratory gathering arranged by Rebecca Sherman, our intrepid Tour manager, at Ozone, a skybar up in the penthouse of the Ritz Carlton, the highest point in Kowloon, to toast our whole extended company and this tour. Excited to see the storied view, we arrive to discover it densely overcast and end up sitting together in middle of a thick cloud with zero visibility. We might as well have been at the bottom of the ocean. But the ludicrousness becomes the focus of our party, just adding fuel to our enjoyment—along with our acknowledgement of this extraordinary tour which is only just getting started. We toast the venture and all involved with a wide array of multi-colored cocktails. When we return to the ground floor to get taxis back to our hotel, only then can we finally see the sparkling overview of this incredible city, and it is glorious.

After the first marathon of Gabriel plays ends on Friday night, Oskar joins Richard for a talk-back. Richard says he's never known of another opportunity like this one he's been given to write the Apple and Gabriel plays—the trust involved. They were far more than a standard commission because, from the outset, they included a commitment of guaranteed productions (and opening dates) at the Public—and all before a word of it had even been written. Oskar also talked passionately about the uniqueness of this extended project, (which he personally enabled) owing especially to the fact that, unlike the way the theater generally works, this project was never 'monetized.' In other words, these plays were not conceived for potential commercial transfer or with even a thought they might make back the money it would cost to produce them, but rather, from the outset, the goal was simply to make art.

Over these last seven years (and across seven countries), the most consistent response we've heard to these seven plays is—'*When are you coming back? We miss you.*' First the Apples, then the Gabriels, became family—initially, to our fellow New Yorkers, and now, to people of various cultures and languages. Family with a capital 'F'. They all wanted to continue to listen in on our conversations. That's what countless people have told us they miss in their own lives. The response from our audiences has been overwhelming; they want us to continue to talk so they can have somewhere safe to sit and reflect with us. I have rarely experienced such passion from audiences, continuing long past the run of the shows. People approach me and Maryann on the street or at the theater when we're attending

Exterior view of the Hong Kong Cultural Centre

Onstage in Hong Kong with Mandarin supertitles *photo: Jeff Harris*

Jay O. Sanders

Page 21

other people's shows. They know our characters. They address us by our characters' names. They *miss our family*. Even in Hong Kong, a man who spoke very little English saw me in the street, pointed, and said 'George?' It was far enough out of context that at first I said, 'Um… no—Jay.' But then he insisted—'George—George Gabriel!' 'Oh, yeah,' I answered. 'Yes, George! I am! And here's Mary, too!' I said as Maryann came walking out of the cafe we'd just been in. 'Mary!!' he exclaimed, thrilled. And despite his difficulty finding the words in English, he pressed on to enthusiastically express, how he had seen us onstage and felt '*I am knowing you.*'

In **Women of a Certain Age**, Mary remembers '*He [Thomas] always said, theater and religion, they were like this…*' (*she interlocks the fingers of both hands to demonstrate they were inextricably connected*). During uncertain times, we need a safe place to gather, listen, and reflect. I remember that feeling very clearly here in New York City in the days immediately following 9/11. We attended a service at our local church for the first time ever, needing to feel the embrace of our community. To know that we were not alone.

> *Zooming in on a white middle-class liberal American household, the drama is more about loss, grief, history, identity and even female intuition, and happens to be set during the months running up to the US presidential election last year…the audience is drawn into their world. The acting is engrossing. The delivery of lines is so spontaneous…that the play appears, at times, almost as if it was unscripted. Nelson's writing is beautiful, poetic and funny.*
>
> Kevin Kwong—*South China Morning Post*

Crossroads of the World at the Big Buddha at Ngong Ping, Lantau Island in Hong Kong

photo: JOS

In front of the Public Theater, 425 Lafayette Street, New York, NY *photo: Amy Warren*

Back to the Public Theater

March 20–24, 2017

THREE WEEKS after we finished in Hong Kong, we all reassembled in LuEsther Hall where the Gabriels were born, to take another important step forward. After a discouraging series of partners falling in and out of making it happen, we finally got a greenlight for WNET to film all three plays here, and as the final piece of the puzzle, Broadway HD came aboard to livestream them all in real time, then archive them for a limited time period before handing the rights back to WNET to re-edit and repackage for airing on PBS. This was a major victory for the project, as it meant there would now be a living record of these plays, demonstrating Richard's vision of the playing style we have developed with him over our time together. What we have created together is not understandable simply through the words of the script, or even a detailed explanation of our rehearsal process and playing experience. My hope is that these filmed versions together with observations like these from our experience living with them, might be useful tools for anyone approaching these plays in the future. The unaffected simplicity we employ is not so much a portrayal as a state of mind. It is carefully-practiced, hard-earned, and often-elusive group work. We are constantly getting notes from Richard, guiding us away from longtime actor habits, preconceptions, and anything presentational. Simple as it may sound, it requires constant reminders, as we have all spent our careers playing by another set of rules.

One great advantage we have in the filming of these plays is that, aside from being asked to wear basically-invisible body mics, nothing we are doing needs to change. David Horn and his *Theater Close-Up/Great Performances* team of producers, camera operators, and technicians (the same group who had filmed all four Apple Family Plays at the Public in the Anspacher Theater in 2013), can come in and simply find us doing what we've been doing all along. And that's what they do. Using six cameras (three set and three mobile), they do their dance with us for an afternoon dress rehearsal and evening livestream, both with invited audiences so the television viewer will always feel the breath and murmur of live theater performance, the importance of which Richard often reflects on within these plays.

The added joy is that this opportunity to preserve these plays comes after we've all had the shared experience of playing in three other houses (on two other continents) to settle into this world together. We're sure to keep growing as we take them on to Europe, but we are in a very relaxed and confident place. There is no such thing as perfection or 'right,' but these films will be a legacy we can be proud of and serve to maintain the vision of this new form. I've often expressed, for the same reason, that I wished we had done a series of interviews with everyone involved in the Apple plays to leave behind with those films. This time, we did. At least minimally. Everyone involved—actors, designers, stage management, technical operators, and of course, Richard—got to talk on camera about the experience of creating and touring The Gabriels. These interviews were then edited into a brief postscript for the *BroadwayHD* broadcast. Hopefully, they can be expanded and used in some way to accompany the PBS version. We now have all seven of Richard's Rhinebeck family plays on film; quite a rare accomplishment in the American theater.

Here now, are some basic acting ground rules for these plays:

- ◆ Make every question a real question; never rhetorical. And always look for the answer in the person you have asked and/or any other character in the room.

- ◆ No conclusions. The point is always to keep the ball in the air, stay curious, and continue to seek forward for more clues. Our company task is to keep the ball in the air throughout the play, so we toss it up, stay engaged, and never let it touch the ground. Keep your head up and always direct your thoughts, no matter how parenthetical, to someone else on stage. Not only does it keep the energy moving forward, but it technically keeps your voice up and out which keeps you generously (and unselfconsciously) audible to the audience, as well as the other actors.

- ◆ A rule for beginning each new scene after a brief time jump; always start in the middle of a thought or story. This goes against our instinct as actors. We are trained to kick up into a new beat or scene, re-energizing the proceedings, but in

Backstage monitor during the livestream and filming of The Gabriels at the Public Theater's LuEsther Hall

photo: JOS

Richard's work the intention is always to be caught midthought which helps keep the dialogue conversational and untheatrical. We must free ourselves of the fear that by not injecting an extra shot of energy we might be boring. The result is that the audience comes to trust us in our truth, because we are not pandering in any way for their attention. I found this difficult for a long time and required regular reminders from Richard before I fully trusted its value. Richard would say, '*let them come and find it for themselves.*' And they always did.

- Avoid anything that smacks of theatrical invention, convention, or pre-thought. '*Dirty it up*,' Richard is fond of saying. Be careful not to fall into patterns of behavior that might suggest this is a rehearsed experience. Therefore, staying as open and responsive as possible, moment to moment through each play, is our constant goal. At the same time, however, we must still be disciplined about adhering to our choices (timing of entrances and exits, for example, and what we have all carefully discussed and agreed must be clearly heard or seen in order for the audience to follow the story) while never pointing to it. It must always feel like real life. It is important for us, as actors, to make sure we connect themes and thoughts in the dialogue, as often an idea is introduced, interrupted, responded to, dropped for a time, then finally answered by some other character. As in life. Stories told in Richard's plays are rarely, themselves, the point of a conversation. The heart of playing them is understanding why that character has chosen to tell a story at that particular moment—sometimes to change the subject from a difficult topic in order to lighten the mood, sometimes to fill time while everyone onstage is waiting for something more important to happen. Richard has often said to me, '*if someone had a more pressing issue to address right now, you would be happy to just drop this story and let things go in that other direction.*' We are surviving by entertaining each other, sharing experiences, lightening the pressures of life at that moment. In **Sweet and Sad** (the second Apple play), for example, we told stories about our 9/11 experiences as a relief from discussing the tragic loss of our niece, Marian's daughter, four months earlier. The more general pain is much easier to face than the immediately personal one. In the next Apple play, **Sorry**, I (as Richard Apple) told a bizarre, true story about the first days of Franklin Pierce's presidency, in order to pass the time before we were scheduled to deliver our Uncle Benjamin to an assisted living facility later that day. They are all gestures of caring for each other, sometimes awkward, sometimes poignant, but always well-intended. In the case of my Sarah Palin story in **That Hopey Changey Thing**, it is a heartfelt appeal to my family to talk, to open ourselves to each other, because that is the bedrock of where we must begin—we need each other. Richard and I have had several conversations about storytelling being the height of optimism. We tell stories because we are exploring who we are. And why and how we live. And the only reason to do that is because we value life itself. A good story-teller is literally 'the life of the party.' And if we hope to find a way to talk as a nation, as a world, we have

Richard Nelson   photo: Maryann Plunkett

to start with the people in our lives we feel safest with and build from there. That thought, that appeal to our better angels, gave rise to the spirit of all seven of the Rhinebeck family plays. Ground rules for why we return to each other for more.

From **Sorry**:

> *The director made a little speech to the actors. The director said—he wanted to be very clear about what they were trying to do. He said—our job—that is, the actors' job—is to put people on the stage who are as complicated, confused, lost, ambiguous, frustrated, uncertain—as any one person in the audience. And then the director said—and of course, we will always fail.*
>
> (an adapted quote from Harley Granville Barker)

Shelly Vance managing the food — photo: Jared Oberholtzer

Susan Hilferty (Costume and Co-Scenic Designer)
photo: Jason Ardizzone-West

Jeremy Adams (General Manager) and Ruth Sternberg (Production Executive)

Jason Ardizzone-West *selfie* (Co-Scenic Designer) — *photo: Hudson Ardizzone-West*

A WORLD IN COMMON *an actor's diary*

Vocally, we play on several levels, as in life, and over time, of course—as with any play—we relaxed into more and more levels, bobbing and weaving in the fits and starts of natural conversation. Primary questions (*Who was on the phone? Is Joyce picking up Mom? What did Paulie say?*), immediate incidental questions (*How thin should I cut this? Do you have any more balsamic? You don't compost?*), parenthetical questions (*Why the fuck can't I remember names anymore?*), and the constant overlaps which occur as we respond to part of someone's question before they've finished their whole thought, sometimes adding our own question, correction, rebuttal, or agreement. These are not angry, impatient overlaps, though, not people trying to keep one another from talking, but rather come out of the enthusiasm of participating fully in the life of the conversation.

So, the spirited nature of our conversations is a reflection of the passion we have to engage with each other. We are not out to convince each other, to make points or mount arguments, but rather, as Richard would constantly remind us—'*the need to talk.*' Often, we would look at each other in the moments before going onstage to start one of the plays and say '*Hey—I need to talk with you!*' The kitchen table is a magnet. We are all relieved to get back to sitting around it, where we know we are welcome, where we can share the burdens of life and feel support and not be alone. And the very act of eating a meal together, or making a meal together, is hopeful, life-affirming; we nourish our bodies and our spirits together as we prepare to face whatever comes next.

Jennifer Tipton (Lighting Designer)
photo: Brigitte Lacombe

Jeff Harris (Tour Production Manager)
photo: Maryann Plunkett

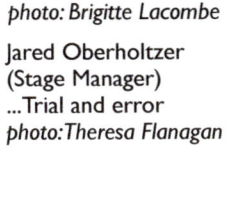

Jared Oberholtzer (Stage Manager) ...Trial and error
photo: Theresa Flanagan

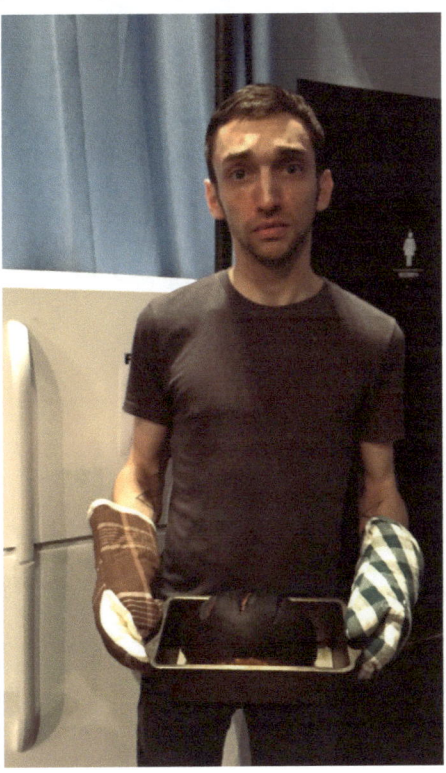

Tess Flanagan (Production Stage Manager) with bread
photo: Jared Oberholtzer

Scott Lehrer (Co-Sound Designer)
photo: Patrick D'Antonio

Jay O. Sanders

Shelly Vance, Lynn Hawley, Roberta Maxwell, Mariam Younes, Maryann Plunkett, Jay O. Sanders, Richard Nelson, Jeff Harris, Rebecca Sherman, Jared Oberholtzer, Laura Brauner, Amy Warren, Tobias Veit, Theresa Flanagan, Meg Gibson

photo: Marija Vahldiek   retouching: Jared Oberholtzer

From Will's sound board at the Schaubühne — photo: Will Pickens

Berlin, Germany

April 15–22, 2017

BERLIN IS a welcoming, livable, and vibrant city. For Richard, Maryann, and me, it holds a special place in our hearts because it was where the whole notion of touring these Rhinebeck plays began. Back in 2013, as we were first putting all four of the Apple plays together for the first time in New York, Tobías Veit, Executive Director of the Schaubühne Theater, looking for interesting new theater on a visit to New York, was guided to see us by his dramaturg Maja Zade. Now, at our 2017 opening night gathering for the Gabriels at the Schaubühne, he recounts the story of having first seen the Apples and being unable to get the experience out of his head for several days. He resolved to meet Richard and find a way to bring this new form of theater to Germany. The first invitation, for that Spring, proved untenable, as some of our cast already had work commitments which conflicted with the dates of their festival. But with Tobías' persistence and creative negotiations a few other festivals joined together, and in the Spring of 2015 we performed our first full marathon—all four Apple plays in one day—at the Schaubühne Festival of International New Drama (FIND). It was the first stop of a tour that would also include international festivals in Brighton, Wiesbaden, and Vienna. But here is where it all began, and the response was immediate. It was the first time we felt the undeniable universality of these plays and the exciting response to the immediacy of this form. And two years later, the Gabriels seem to have brought our work even closer.

Our first night in Berlin—that very first night—we are invited to attend the dress rehearsal of a play written and directed by a well-known theater maker from Madrid, Angélica Liddell, titled *Dead Dog at Dry*

Cleaners. Only a few of us feel up to it after the long flight. It features members of the Schaübuhne's resident acting company and is a striking example of a form of theater diametrically opposed to everything we are doing. It has nudity, simulated rape, a repetition of words or phrases matched with extreme physical gestures, smashed furniture (five or six chairs were methodically broken up with axes, while another was simply thrown against a wall), and lots of running literally in circles while lines and quotes from classic literature are shouted loudly. The actors face front, scream at the audience, insulting us and challenging us to leave. At one point they stare at us for several silent, defiant minutes). All performed with admirable commitment and athleticism. Ms. Liddell describes her work as *Poetry that Smashes Our Comfort*. Our plays and hers are a stark study in stylistic contrasts.

The whole acting company of the Schaubühne, many of whom had been on vacation when the Apples had played here two years before, were all now encouraged to attend the Gabriels. Artistic director Thomas Ostermeier said repeatedly, *'We have to find a way to bring what you are doing into our own work.'* On Sunday night, after our final marathon in which we were brought back for five curtain calls, Thomas and Tobías arrived at our dressing rooms, clearly deeply moved, repeating this sentiment once again. *'How are you doing this—keeping so much focus for all these hours? We need to learn this!'* Hearing this from one of the premiere stage directors of the modern German theater was particularly meaningful. We were obviously making our mark. And particularly now, as the whole world watched the daily adrenalized tweetstorm and chaotic deluge of wrecking-ball executive orders from the White House, we were providing a very different face for our country; human, accessible, and as confused as everyone else about where we were all headed. Ambassadors.

Decisive political theater always runs the risk of being instructive or cabaret…The danger of the cabaret is that it is jokes exclusively for the like-minded. One remains comfortable among themselves. I think theater is political when it comes to asking questions and there are no answers. If it formulates contradictions, but does not dissolve them. And if we can see the seemingly familiar world anew. For me, this [The Gabriels] is very illuminating political theater.

Peter Carp—Badische Zeitun

Schaubühne Theater charts and photos, showing the flexibility of their three main spaces

photo: Jeff Harris

Timecapsule

Over the course of the year since our tour, as I've organized this book, allowing time for reflection, editing, and the gathering of reviews and photos, Richard's work (and mine with him) has continued. Looking back, I am struck by how many critics across the world made comparisons to Chekhov. Appropriately, our next project together—in the winter of 2018—was his brand new co-translation of *Uncle Vanya*. Somehow, during the six weeks between our Gabriel bookings in Berlin and Brighton, Richard had taken the time to go to Paris and collaborate for the seventh time with two of the world's foremost translators of Russian literature, Larissa Volokhonsky and Richard Pevear. Our producer this time was Barry Edelstein, who had run the Shakespeare Initiative and Lab conservatory at the Public Theater during our first years of the Apples, and for the last five years, has been artistic director of San Diego's Old Globe Theater. And again, Richard directed.

I was excited to be offered the role of Vanya and joined a company of actors who had also worked with Richard many times before, including castmates from the Gabriels (Roberta Maxwell), the Apples (Jon DeVries and Jesse Pennington) and various other productions (Yvonne Woods, Kate Kearney-Patch, and Celeste Arias). It seemed imperative that we finally apply this style we had been building together to Chekhov, to see how it sat with the work of the man who had inspired so much of it. Yet another experiment. And according to both critics and audiences—it seemed to work.

Quietly arresting—a beautifully rewarding exploration.
James Hebert, *San Diego Union-Tribune*

It's important to be on the watch for definitive productions as well as breakthroughs. This Uncle Vanya will henceforth have an important place in my Chekhov Wing.
Welton Jones, *San Diego Story*

This new Vanya has a conversational smoothness that removes the cobwebs...every minute is imbued with a density of life...lovers of Chekhov have cause for celebration: This is one of the most exquisite renderings of Uncle Vanya I've encountered, a heartbreaking reading of the play that retains just enough of the original's sly humor to be truly Chekhovian...Nelson's strengths as a director lead him to the heart of what makes Vanya such an enduring work of dramatic literature. The character relationships are laid bare with the speed and dexterity needed to bring forth Chekhov's compassionate vision of the human condition.
Charles McNulty, *L.A. Times*, February 20, 2018

And once we had opened *Vanya*, Richard returned to Paris with the Pevears, emerging with a new translation of Chekhov's *Three Sisters*.

The Outsiders

IN ALL seven of these Rhinebeck plays, the outsiders are a very important element, both catalysts and witnesses.

In the Apples, two of the six characters are Apple siblings visiting from New York City, who need to be filled in on recent family events. Another outsider is sister Jane's new younger actor boyfriend, Tim, who has heard her stories about the family but is otherwise fresh to their lives. His presence allows Richard an ally onstage to talk about the nature of Theater itself. An avidly curious admirer of Uncle Benjamin's lifetime body of work, Tim opens several doors leading to information, theory, and even revelation, questioning Benjamin, for example, about the effect of his memory loss on his identity as an actor.

In the Gabriels, the matriarch, Patricia (played by Roberta Maxwell) has just recently become an outsider from her own kitchen, as she has moved herself into a local retirement home. She brings news and curiosity to the table from across town. Things are often explained to the outsiders out of necessity. City mouse/Country mouse jokes, misunderstandings, and underlying family resentments fuel the conversation. (Chekhov is full of similar examples, as well; those who know Moscow and the outside world alternately fascinate and rub up against those in the country who don't.) Theater is represented by Joyce, a professional associate costume designer (Amy Warren in our production) and Karin, an out-of-work actor (Meg Gibson). An occasional visitor up from the City, Joyce's international travels have to be worked around in order for family gatherings to be possible. Karin has just taken a job in the area teaching playwriting at an upscale private school to survive. She is Thomas' first wife (there were three) from 35 years earlier and has not been back since the break-up, aside from a recent visit to see Thomas, at his request, near the very end of his life. In **Hungry**, she finds herself in the area, by chance, on the day of the scattering of his ashes and is invited along by his widow and third wife, Mary (Maryann Plunkett). The mystery of her presence ripples through the plays and provides someone of the Theater (Thomas' world) to whom the family's situation must be explained as things unfold. As with Tim, in the Apples, she importantly becomes an outside conduit through which the audience can enter the Gabriels' world, providing someone in the room who is curious and lacks the others' unspoken history. Over the course of the cycles of the Apples and Gabriels, both Tim and Karin gradually become part of the family, just as the audience does. They are a gift to the dramatist and the audience, as it is the distance between them and the families which continuously enables the interactions onstage, unearthing insights, information, and revelations. Were it not for the presence of the outsiders, the audience would find it much more difficult to find their way to the table.

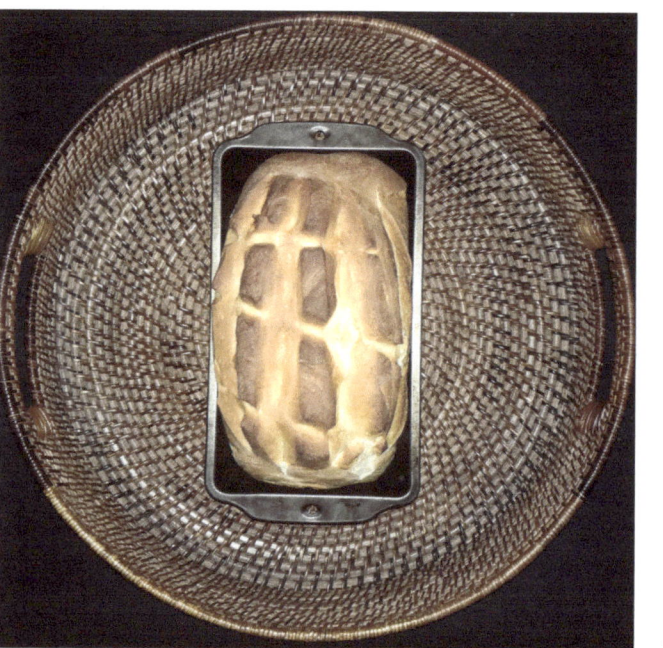

photo: Jared Oberholtzer

Brighton, UK

May 14–28, 2017

AGAIN, SOME of us are back in familiar territory. There is a whole audience here who remember the Apples from 2015, only days before their own election, which proved to be a shocking upset of the favored Liberal Party. I have managed to continue my travel ineptness by losing a container which held all my credit cards (and my passport card!) somewhere along the way. As with my passport en route to Australia, this is the first time I've ever done this, despite a lifetime of travel. I quickly had the cards cancelled and replacements were on their way as soon as I discovered them missing, but still, it was disconcerting.

Attenborough Centre for the Creative Arts (BCCA), Sussex University near Brighton © RH Partnership

Last time we were here, we stayed in the Victorian-era Old Ship Hotel right on the seaside, overlooking the long pebble beach and famous Brighton Pier. This time, we experience a very different side of Brighton. We find ourselves across from the train station, in a hotel with its lobby under reconstruction. Throughout the day, drills and metal saws loudly surprise us. One morning, the smell of glue used in the laying down of tiles greets us in the dining room off the lobby during breakfast. We grin and bear it, but it clearly will not be one of the more comfortable hotel experiences of this tour. Since the Corn Exchange next to the Brighton Dome—the theater where we performed last time—is also in the process of reconstruction, we will be playing in a brand-new theater at Sussex University, a 20-minute train ride away in Falmer.

Even before we arrived in Brighton, we'd already been touted as the must-see theater event of the festival by a critic from The Stage (a major

UK theater publication) on the strength of the impression we had made here with the Apples in 2015. Michael Billington, one of the most respected of the London theater critics, had also been deeply impressed on that visit, giving our four-play cycle a rare five-star review in The Guardian. Various theater professionals we encountered in London after the Apple week were buzzing about it, frustrated that his review had come out the same day as our final marathon, so by then there had been no chance for any of them to run down and catch it. So, the anticipation of our traveling company's arrival at the Brighton Festival gives us something to live up to.

The new theater, the Attenborough Centre for the Creative Arts, is a round-shaped building with a central dome over the audience and a raised proscenium stage in its own housing just off the circular shape. For our purposes, however, we've brought the audience onto the stage with us, placing seating units on either side and pulled the theater's normal seating forward to create our kitchen playing area. However, with our adjustment, we've pulled the central seating unit forward, altering its relation to the dome's acoustic design. We now find ourselves facing a serious echo problem for the back five rows of the center section. And they can't hear us! Obviously, this will be disastrous if it can't be solved.

We are confronted with an acoustical nightmare and a very brief time in which to solve it and recalibrate our dynamic together. On top of this, it's now been six weeks since we last actually performed these plays. And now I'm told (privately, as most in the cast do not wish to know) that for some reason, most of the critics have been invited to our first marathon—our very first day of performances—rather than giving us at least a day or two to find our footing back with an audience. Oh yes…and that will include *'the London critics'*—meaning Mr. Billington from The Guardian will be back, as well as various others. It is, to say the least—especially given Richard's long history and reputation here in England—a challenging

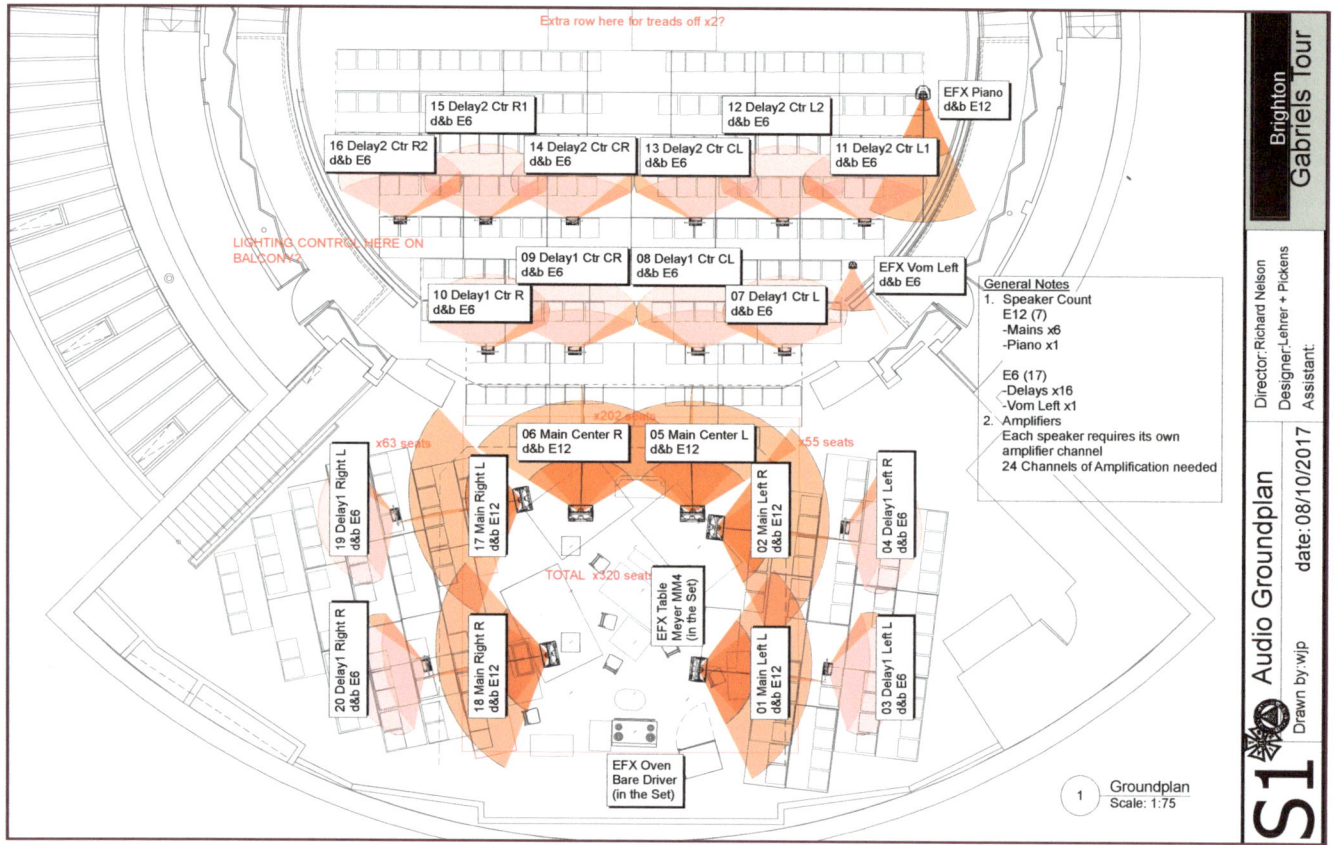

Will's drawings showing onstage seating units and strategic speaker placement

photo: Will Pickens

scenario. We all want to represent this extraordinary work at the high level it deserves. Nothing to be done but take hands and jump.

Fortunately, our traveling sound team, Will and Laura, working with a very game and efficient stage crew, led by Beth Carrington (the same tech director who had stepped up to save the day in 2015 for the Apples) who had since moved over to run this theater and understands what we're doing. With only two days for tech rehearsals, they finally hang 'blacks' (thick black theater curtains) around the upper reaches of the dome's center, including laying them along the floors of the catwalks overhead, substantially deadening much of the afflicting echo and audibility issue. The cast all focuses on our part—not volume, because louder sounds actually echo more, but intention, as Richard observes. We must keep our speaking clear—consonants, not dropping ends of words, and avoiding breathiness—and focused out to whomever we're speaking. It is a delicate business, but together we find our way to a comfortable playing level, and the rehearsals are remarkably fresh and alive. Our marathon will be the first time since Berlin (again, six weeks ago) that we'll be working with props, costumes, food…and, of course, audience.

Miraculously, the first marathon is an unqualified, almost otherworldly success. With every department on point and focused together, we experience a totally engaged, intelligent audience, leaning in to be at the kitchen table with us for all three plays. Unforced reactions ripple around the theater throughout the day, and finally we are greeted with a standing ovation full of heart; nodding heads, loud exclamations, and many tear-stained faces. We are all here together and connected beyond words. They are knowing us.

Will Pickens listens and fine tunes from above   photo: JOS

Challenges of the road also include illness. And without understudies, we are on delicate ground. Everyone's health must be guarded. Soon after that first marathon on Saturday, our matriarch, Roberta Maxwell/Patricia Gabriel, feels something serious going on with her throat, so we hurry back to the hotel as directly as possible to allow her the maximum rest, in anticipation of another three-show day on Sunday. A collection of pharmaceuticals, teas, and steamers are taken up to her new room (where she's just been moved because she had no hot water!). Even so, by Sunday morning Roberta has no voice. Telephones are abuzz looking for a doctor, but neither the Brighton Festival physician nor anyone else—it being a bank holiday—can be found. Our wonderful Tour Manager, Rebecca Sherman, accompanies Roberta to a local clinic where they wait for awhile until they learn it will be another 3½ hours before she can be seen, so they return to the hotel, distraught. I share with her an emergency tactic I learned years ago when I found myself in a similar spot, relayed to me from a friend's opera singer sister. Soak a paper towel in cooking oil, wrap it around your neck and cover it with plastic-wrap for maximum insulation, then put a towel snugly over that, so as to insulate and heat the area up. She tries it—along with everything else she's been given—and we forge ahead with the show, fingers crossed. At the very worst, we figure we know her lines well enough that we can repeat things she tries to say or fill in gaps of information needed for the scene to happen. If it's impossible after that, the decision will have to be made as to whether we cancel the other two shows. She makes her 11th hour entrance in **Hungry**, making a 'holy shit, here we go' face at me before we come on together, I say my first line, her cue, she opens her mouth to answer…and *'I just remembered it,'* she says clearly, *'I don't know why….?'* Her eyes light up in delight as she looks back at me—Oh my god—a voice! A little iffy perhaps, but definitely there and actually perfect for someone who has just woken up (which is even remarked on in the scene). She is terrific. And from there, she makes her way through the whole day, to great elation from all of us! The marathon is another memorable experience—the audience again jumps to their feet at the end of the last play and again their faces are full of tears, smiles, and bravos. Now we have until Tuesday night to rest, and only **Hungry** that night—her lightest show. Old, dear friends of hers who live down the coast are waiting there for her after the marathon ends to collect her in their car and whisk her away for a couple days of chicken soup, acupuncture, and sea air!

The next night, England is rocked by a suicide bombing in Manchester, targeting young people at an Ariana Grande concert. More than 20 people die and several are wounded, shocking the world and especially this country. It was the deadliest attack in the United Kingdom since the July 7, 2005 bombing in London. There is a scramble to make sure the authorities know the full extent of who was involved and whether or not there might be more ahead. Two days later, Theresa May raises the threat level to *'critical'* for the first time since 2007. Despite the perfect weather here in Brighton, the mood on the streets is subdued.

During the three individual shows this week, we continue to feel a sadness from the houses, an unsettledness. It is reminiscent of the week after the election back in November, we feel a renewed sense of purpose to create a gathering place for a community in need of human contact and reflection. These audiences are more sober than the weekend, slower to embrace the comedy of the plays, but very fully present and attentive. And we can still feel them breathing with us. Our function as ambassadors of humanity is felt by us all. In all of my years as an actor, I have never heard so many people characterize an experience as 'one of the most memorable experiences of their lives.' And given the particularly communal nature of what we are doing, it doesn't go to our heads as much as to our hearts. The unpresented style, the simple truth we engage, and the reflection of what it means to be alive in this world right now has continued to ring out loud and clear in each successive venue, but somehow here it has intensified.

Then, our final marathon arrives. Saturday. And once again, the houses are less like audience than extended family. And the responses, during and after, are profound. As a cast, we continue to stay open to each new day, forgetting as much as possible so we can discover things as they happen; keeping it fresh. News passes through the backstage of a serious IT problem which has hit the whole British Airways computer system, causing massive cancellations and chaos, especially at Heathrow—the very airport and airline we're scheduled to fly out of and on tomorrow afternoon to Hamburg.

> **The unpresented style, the simple truth we engage, and the reflection of what it means to be alive in this world right now has continued to ring out loud and clear in each successive venue, but somehow here it has intensified.**

In the meantime, the producers of the Brighton Festival have contacted Maryann about stepping in last-minute to read the classic oration that accompanies Aaron Copland's *Lincoln Portrait* at the Dome Theater for the Festival's closing concert, replacing Fiona Shaw who has become unavailable. It is an extraordinary opportunity to bring this great American's inspiring voice of sanity to an international audience in these strange political times. They offer to keep both of us here in our hotel another night, then fly us on to Hamburg early Monday morning out of Gatwick Airport to join our group. It is too exciting a chance to pass up, and the adjustment is made.

The rest of our company, however, is now feeling all sorts of anxiety about the British Airways/Heathrow situation. Richard, Jeff, and Will need to be at the Hamburg theater space at 8 am Monday to evaluate the space and adjust the exact placement of the Gabriel kitchen set pieces for sightlines which, in turn, will dictate the placement of Jeff's lights and Will's microphones. The timing of all this is paramount because we are scheduled to perform **Hungry** for our first audience on Tuesday night! So, those three (and a couple of others) are weighing the options of a long but dependable train ride as a possible alternative to the present unsureness of the air travel. Our tour manager, Rebecca, has begun to receive reassuring reports from our group's travel agent that flights are starting to take off from Heathrow, but a lack of faith in the airline's assurances leaves the train travelers to continue to question official reports. It's decided to save their decision for the morning. The rest will meet in the lobby for a 10 am pickup.

In the end, five decide to head off for the train alternative but, thanks to more online confusion, end up joining the rest at Heathrow for the original flight, and they all take off together only an hour later than originally planned. Crisis averted.

That evening, Maryann takes the stage at the Brighton Dome to close the festival and delivers an inspiring rendition of the *Lincoln Portrait* accompanied by the Britten Sinfonia, an internationally-acclaimed chamber orchestra, as a 250-member chorus sits just upstage, listening, and waiting for their piece in the second half. She manages to stay strong and clear, even through—*a government of the people by the people, for the people*—celebrating the ideals of our U.S. Constitution, as the painful irony in this time of alternative facts hangs thickly in the air. After the concert, we attend a champagne reception to toast the performance and the end of the Brighton Theater Festival.

The next morning, we are picked up very early to catch our flight to join the rest of the company. Our stage manager, Tess Flanagan, has gotten in touch with me because she left her iPhone in the lobby, and it's waiting at the front desk. I retrieve it and pack it carefully in my carry-on to keep it safe.

Waiting in Hamburg Airport for our flight to Amsterdam—*left to right:* Will Pickens, Jared Oberholtzer, Cindy Nelson, Richard Nelson, Heather Fichthorn, Laura Brauner, Theresa Flanagan, Shelly Vance

photo: Maryann Plunkett

...a theatrical miracle...one of the loveliest and most profound things I have ever seen...a way of understanding people by looking and listening very hard...But what is so extraordinary and so moving...is that the actual experience of watching the plays embodies this theory. Because nothing seems to be happening, except a family coming together and making a meal, the audience leans forward to listen, intently picking up every word...you become part of the family, sharing their hopes and fears, laughing at their jokes (the plays are extremely funny) and admiring their stoical refusal to give up or be bowed down...They embody the empathy they preach thanks to performances that go so far beyond naturalism that you feel the actors are just living the lives they are imagining...not a depressing thing, however. They are survivors, jumping across the abyss, with love and hope in their hearts. As an audience, the amount you care about them is a tribute to the power of theatre itself. It really is nothing and everything, a story and an entire world. Unforgettable.

Sarah Crompton—Brighton: What'sOnStage (5 out of 5 stars)

...an extraordinary theatrical event in which the personal and the political combine in a way that suggests a contemporary Chekhov. These plays are specifically American, but they touch on universal questions. They also raise one of the biggest issues in the UK election: the problem of paying for social care. Nelson writes with compassion and insight about those left behind by American money worship and, while the hyperrealism of his production means you don't catch every word, his actors brilliantly inhabit his characters. "What the hell happened to history?" one character enquires, referring to the shameless commercialisation of the local Roosevelt Museum. One answer is that it is being recorded by Nelson in these deeply moving portraits of the dissolving American dream.

Michael Billington—The Guardian (5 out of 5 stars)

Production Assistant, Joseph Fernandez, with bread
photo: Jared Oberholtzer

Richard Nelson's trilogy is a quietly stunning masterpiece of understated naturalism. The three plays... unmask the fractured face of contemporary America with breath-taking articulacy...By the end of the third play, after five-and-a-half hours of supremely understated drama, Nelson's characters don't feel like friends, they feel like family...Nelson's clockwork theatre ventures beyond naturalism, into uber-naturalism. He out-Chekhovs Chekhov, and his six-strong cast—he directs as well—are flawless. It seems wrong to single anyone out in such a universally polished ensemble...There's politics here too, but of a subtler, slower kind...And in this restraint, in this downbeat refinement, Nelson finds a thrilling power...He wrote these plays prior to Trump's election, and they have only grown in resonance since then. The trilogy encapsulates a country from the kitchen table. It's everyday. It's epic. And it's a quietly stunning theatrical achievement.

Fergus Morgan—The Stage (5 out of 5 stars)

...its miraculous, almost invisible craft...restores full humanity to a family of lower-middle class Americans who often feel slighted and helpless...The Gabriels' social support, intimate warmth and spontaneous humour—and these are very funny plays—keep them fighting their losing battles.

Nick Hasted—The Arts Desk (5 out of 5 stars)

...a huge achievement...an astonishingly—and I mean astonishingly—lifelike replication of the ebb and flow, herk and jerk, fondness and bitterness of real-life conversation. How good is the acting? Well, Meg Gibson, Lynn Hawley, Roberta Maxwell, Jay O Sanders, Maryann Plunkett and Amy Warren all convince you that they are just living, not acting. That's how good it is. I don't think I'll ever forget the sad, funny, political, deeply intelligent and richly human day I spent with the Gabriels.

Dominic Maxwell—The Times (4 out of 5 stars)

Hamburg, Germany

May 29–June 5, 2017

Kampnagel, former crane factory, now home to six theater spaces — photo: JOS

Rehearsing in Hamburg, as we try to solve the challenging sound situation — photo: Jeff Harris

MARYANN AND I arrive from Brighton to discover that the young intern who is to pick us up isn't there. I call the number I've been given for her and am met with a confused reaction. *'Oh no—I had a later time listed for your arrival.'* She tells us she's half an hour away, so we settle in at a Starbucks across from the baggage claim to wait, corralling our bags around a couple of comfortable chairs, as we get ourselves something to drink. When she arrives, she's sweet and very apologetic about the mix-up as we take our bags out to her van.

It takes us half an hour to get where we're staying, and as we roll our bags toward the front door of the hotel, I offer to take one of Maryann's bags for her, as she has two to worry about and I've only got…oh shit! I suddenly realize that I only have one bag. I've somehow managed to leave my carry-on bag—with my computer, iPad, headphones…and of course, Tess's iPhone!—back at the airport! Shit! Shit!! Shit!!!

I quickly call our driver and manage to catch her as she is just about to return to the airport to pick up someone else, so she swings back around and picks me up. As we drive, I nervously joke with her that, given people's present level of anxiety, it's probably already been found and destroyed with a controlled explosion. The second we arrive, I jump out and go directly to the Starbucks seating area which is now completely filled with people…but no sign of my bag. I ask one of the servers behind the counter if a black rolling bag has been turned in. She replies 'no' and guides me to the Airport Information Desk just down the hall. No black bag has been turned in to them, either, but the woman I speak to sends me to security back in the baggage claim area. Once there, I am told they only handle lost checked bags and am directed back to the same desk I had just spoken to—the same ones who had sent me here. But I do it, anyway, just for somewhere to go.

The answer is still the same, but the woman asks me to write down my information and promises to get it to me when it shows up. She is very reassuring about it, but somehow I feel I've hit a dead end. I ask if there is somewhere I can charge my cell phone—it's almost completely dead—and she points to a small socket across the hall near the floor. I plug in my phone with the charger, and stand there as it charges, wracking my brain for specific images of where I left my bag. Standing there, I notice the people going by; happily-reunited families, flight attendants, and young soldiers in uniform carrying machine guns. I wonder if this is the new normal here or have they just been assigned to patrol here in response to the heightened alert since Manchester. I decide to ask the woman at the info desk one last time and retrace my steps for her. This time, she jumps up out of her seat, saying *'Starbucks? I will check at the Starbucks! We have had many bags left there before.'* And she heads quickly off down the hall to check. As I return to my phone, still sitting out on the floor charging, I see the woman from the info desk coming quickly back toward me, her face is now ashen.

'Your bag—does it have a blue, um…'

'Ribbon?—a blue ribbon on the handle, yes!' I ask. 'You found it?'

'They have found it there, yes. You must go quickly there and talk to them.'

I grab my phone and charger and head down the hall to where I can see six security officers, including the two who had passed me earlier with machine guns. They have cordoned off the Starbucks seating area, cleared the immediate area, and I see my bag sitting out in the center of the open space.

'This is yours?' the main officer asks, pointing.

'Yes, that's mine, with the blue ribbon, yes!'

The officer in charge shakes his head. *'This is very bad. Do you know?'*

'Yes, I know—I certainly didn't mean to leave it. It has my computer in it and everything.'

Again, he shakes his head. *'Very bad. Given all what has been going on.'*

'I know. Trust me—I know. I'm from New York.'

'New York?' he pauses for a moment, looks at me, then says, *'Ah… the Big Apple!'*

'Yeah.'

'Your computer? You can tell me where is it?'

'Outer pocket, second set of zippers. I keep it in a cover that looks like a book. It's got a red binding.'

Moving to it cautiously, he slowly unzips that pocket…and sure enough, the red binding pokes out. As he looks more closely, a more senior officer approaches, skeptically taking in me and the scene. The two of them confer, shake their heads, then finally nod at me and they all relax and move away; the High Alert is over. I take my bag, get in a taxi, and head back to the hotel, in serious need of a shower to reset.

After an imperative nap, I notice a text Rebecca sent me a couple of hours earlier, inviting us out to watch Richard 'perform' at a special festival installation at the harbor. A temporary village has been created by festival-related artists, including one who has built a small wooden house where he has been living for the last five days with enough room for about twenty people to sit and watch him in conversation with specially invited guests. We jump in a taxi with possibly the most timid driver we've ever encountered who proceeds to give us a whispered tour of everything we pass, moving way too carefully, turning the wheel in small jerky hand motions, as though he's still just learning to drive, but eventually we make our way down to the harbor. *'We're having drinks on a boat, come join us!'* Rebecca writes. Maryann and I wander through this intriguing configuration of tents, warehouses, food trucks, laid-out grassy areas, and colorful festival signs…not a clue—*'Which boat?'* I text back, when suddenly we see waving from way up on the deck on an old freighter that seems to have been repurposed here. We climb the long gangplank to find a few members of our group (including Tess, newly reunited with her iPhone) having a glass of wine with Richard and his wife, Cindy, post-*'performance.'* Apparently, it was all very interesting (though very hot inside) and the recap we get by Richard and the others is entertaining enough to make us feel a part of it all despite coming late to the party. A few of us stick around the makeshift village to dine on a mix of vegetable curries, beer, wine, and exotic sausages from various vendors. Hello, Hamburg!

Our theater is in a whole different part of town, set within an enormous, repurposed factory/warehouse called Kampnagel—Germany's largest independent production venue for the performing arts, a former mechanical engineering factory where huge cranes for construction and ship-loading were built. The ceilings are 40 or 50 feet high in places, and houses six different flexible theater spaces (as well as scenery/prop shops and lighting storage). It is an experimental theater maker's dream space; literally anything is possible. The hard part, however, (certainly in our space) is—once again—managing the sound. As with a converted church space, the resulting echoes are unavoidable. Having just conquered the 'impossible' situation in Brighton, our team arrives boldly and optimistically to the challenge. There are some black curtains hung behind one section, but it only accounts for about a third of the room. Two more

are hung on either side, behind our side audiences, but still, the sound bounce when facing to the back is considerable. So, Richard, Will, and Laura Brauner (our ever-present live sound mixer) go about the process of figuring it out. After working through scenes and addressing one discovery at a time, we become aware that the louder we talk, the harder it is to understand us, because we activate the echoes and make the dialogue muddy. And my voice, specifically, when I speak in my lower register, is like playing a bass drum under a bridge. So, what's the solution? First off, we all find a common volume level that works just below the echo line, give greater attention to our consonants and ends of lines, and, most importantly, direct every single thing we say to the person we're saying it to—once again, intention is all. Will and Laura are then able to lift that clear sound enough with the mikes for the audience to hear and understand it. And I have the highly unusual task of playing all three plays without using my bottom octave. If we weren't so at home with these plays now, this could be a soul-killing adjustment, making us all so self-conscious as to defeat the entire spirit of these plays. But instead, given everything we've been through together, the challenge is immediately embraced by the group. We can do this. We are warned that our first performance that night, **Hungry**, may be rather lightly attended, but instead, it is practically full, and step by step, scene by scene, we find our way through this new tuning. They are a very quiet house. We're aware that many of them seem to be reading the supertitles, (provided for us here by Jacob, our affable young collaborator from the Schaubühne) which makes it harder to gauge how they are receiving us. On top of that, the theater has gotten very hot. A few people leave, but those who are here seem very attentive. At the end, as with Brighton's more subdued audiences during last week, they explode with applause and cheers, calling us back for two extra curtain calls and the festival producer bringing us all flowers. We have once again found the Gabriels' kitchen and our family connection under the echo sound ceiling, a whole new experience in adaptability. I am very proud of our ensemble and entire team tonight on a whole new level.

On our day off, Maryann and I take a two-hour boat tour which gives us a relaxing overview of the city. We glide across the lake and out into the network of ubiquitous canals around and through Hamburg. We are treated to the beautiful architecture (a city rebuilt after WWII with a clever use of glass overstructures, creating new hybrid spaces, which marry modern design with the structural details and integrity of war-damaged older buildings), the celebrated new Philharmonic concert hall, and even pass by the factory where our theater is..

Our first Hamburg marathon. After a week of perfect walking weather (sunny with cooling breezes), as if on cue for spending the day indoors, it rains. The audience is only at about half, but they tuck down close around us, creating a wonderful sense of intimacy. The first show plays fine, but we are not yet fully on our game together after a day off. There is a bit of backsliding in the delicate business of trusting this new playing level. The audience—again, most of them reading along as they watch—still seem to connect very strongly, as confirmed by the strong response at the first curtain call (even though the first two bows are more of formality, a courtesy we have practiced during the marathons)—bringing us back for a second call, even this early in the day. But we all feel the need to re-find our stride together. And with the next two shows, we do.

As I sit backstage (here, that means underneath the central seating unit), I become aware of a strange new element on the soundtrack; birds. The closer I listen, the louder they get, and I begin to wonder if this is some unusual new artsy layer of Rhinebeck that Will has begun added into the background. When I ask him about it later, he says, 'Yeah—isn't it amazing! But no, I didn't do it—it's from outside the theater. The birds here are just that loud!!'

At the second show, once again, the intensity of the audience's engagement with us is palpable. They are at our table with us, living these plays; the magic of what Richard has created with us. We are in a universal kitchen, making meals and conversation to sustain, simultaneously, a very specific and an archetypal family. And today, Hamburg is Rhinebeck.

These weekend marathons are the most sparsely attended shows of our tour, ranging from about 100 people the first day to only about 60 the second, but fierce listeners, with us every step, so the numbers don't matter. As before, every play gets enthusiastic applause and a second call, culminating in loud cheering, group foot-stomping (typical here), and multiple calls with everyone rising to their feet by the third call. We continue to make our mark.

> *...one of the highlights of the "Theater of the World" festival... something happens to the viewer...He climbs into their family cosmos and their problems, which could occur everywhere... Richard Nelson...does not want to teach. In times of ambiguity, worries, fears and general confusion, he would like to name these. Nelson sees the theater as a "place of ritual", which is nothing less than humanity.*
>
> Annette Stiekele—*Hamburger Abendblatt*

Amsterdam, Holland

June 5–12, 2017

The Gabriels set up in the Tobacco Theater Frascati in Amsteram photo: JOS

Old photograph of the Tobacco Exchange in the same space as our theater

THE HOLLAND Festival is one of the oldest, largest theater festivals in the world, and this year it is bigger than ever. In celebration of their 70th year of existence, fifty separate theater, dance, and opera productions are being presented. Our performance space is in a building that goes back to the 1600s which had, at one time, been a monastery, an inn, and finally, the Tobacco Exchange, before becoming a performance space now known simply as *'Frascati.'* When we all first arrive, we are overjoyed to find that it is remarkably reminiscent of our original home at the Public, LuEsther Hall. We are also ecstatic to find, after our experiences in Hamburg and Brighton, that the sound here is extremely friendly to our voices and the warm glow of the light bouncing off the deep brown hardwood floors gives the feel of an old house. This will be a perfect space to finish our tour and the 16 months we have spent as the Gabriels. We are home. On top of that, we are told that all three of our marathons are effectively sold out.

We work one long, intense day, teching and running all three shows, still rehearsing them at the same intensity we have maintained since we began. We continue to attend to details, relationships, clarity, needing to talk to each other, and never knowing what's going to happen. This is an extraordinary group of artists where no one is *'over it'* or coasting through to the end. Now, we have a day off to wander and relax here in preparation for our final weekend of nine shows in three days. So, let the games begin!

Our day off takes us to the impressive Van Gogh Museum, the Anne Frank House, and the Rembrandt House. Reminiscent of Hamburg, we take glass-covered canal boat rides, explore cheese shops, bakeries, bookstores, and flea markets. Bicycles everywhere, we get around on trains and buses, get strong whiffs of weed as we walk by rows of 500-year-old buildings, we visit the Opera House and pass Ivo Van Hove's theater (his National Theater production of *Obsession* and opera of *Salome* are part of the festival).

Thursday, June 8th is also the day of the UK elections—a specially-called vote by Prime Minister Theresa May to shore up her majority in Parliament in support of her Brexit initiatives. Despite projections of a possible landslide in her favor, May actually loses her majority and is faced with completely rethinking and reorganizing the balance of the government. Also, today, in Washington D.C., the controversially-dismissed head of the FBI, James Comey, testifies publically in front of a Senate Committee making strong claims against President Trump, accusing him of lying, slandering the FBI, and repeatedly applying inappropriate pressures on him (Comey) relating to the ongoing investigations about allegations of collusion between Trump's campaign and Russia. Trump retaliates in kind the next day, accusing Comey of lying about everything and offers to make his own sworn testimony to that effect. We are all very glad to be away from the center of this ongoing political shitstorm.

Marathon 1

The latest start we've had—first show, 3 pm, the last at 9. The first 20 minutes is intense listening, as the audience adjusts to our American English and this style of performance which is completely foreign to them in the theater. Somewhere about fifteen to twenty minutes in, we can feel them relaxing, accepting what we're doing, and starting to respond more freely. Given the rhythm of their response, it also seems to suggest a combination of listening and reading supertitles, but they are right with us.

In this friendly space, we find our stride together as actors right away. The shows are very alive with many new discoveries and surprises throughout. At the end of **Hungry**, the audience applauds, but politely, giving a very measured response. The same after **What Did You Expect?,** belying how involved we can clearly feel they are. It seems to be a taste of Dutch reserve. But when Mary leaves the stage at the end of **Women of a Certain Age**, the reserved façade falls away. They all rise to their feet in rapid succession and become very vocal in their appreciation. At our second call, beautiful bouquets of fresh flowers are brought out to each of us by representatives of the Holland Festival, and we then join in the applause—from us to them. Afterwards, our producers give us a special toast in the bar/café located in the same building. As Richard and I are talking together, we are approached by

Judy McFarland (Wardrobe Supervisor) with bread

the artistic director of a theater in Antwerp, Belgium who had seen the Apples in Vienna two years ago and now The Gabriels here today, and she wants The Gabriels to come to her theater next year. *'This is a conversation we need to be having,'* she insists. *'Especially with an American company, to be talking about these things and to hear your voice.'* Jeremy Adams joins the conversation, and Richard introduces him as *'an important figure in our group—our main tour producer from the Public—who truly understands the value of what we are doing.'* Richard tells the Belgian director that unfortunately this weekend is the end of our tour, explaining the difficulties these days of maintaining any kind of company in our country, as even most of the regional theater companies that once existed have disbanded. He explains that even having kept this small group of six actors together for a year and a half is some kind of miracle. The Public Theater has given us a home and support but they are a very large organization and are already on to launching many other projects now. He says he believes, however, that the touring format, the idea of having a successful ongoing conversation with the world through art, is the way of the future for artists like us, whose goal has always been first and foremost to be part of a continuing dialogue through our work, rather than the pursuit of commercial success. The artistic director from Antwerp is passionate and persistent about wanting to stay in touch about whatever project we are doing next. And so, our dream of an emerging touring matrix continues to grow.

Marathon 2

Maryann and I walked to the theater today, along the canals past houseboats of all shapes and sizes. It's a beautiful day and everyone is out. A man feeds a flock of pigeons with an oddly methodical calm, looking up at us with a gentle smile as we pass, that makes us both comment it looks as though he's been doing this regularly for decades. We pass the Amsterdam wing of the Russian Hermitage Museum, then the opera house and another theater—which are both hosting various international productions as part of our Holland Festival. We cross a bridge with a plaque noting a memorial for 200 Jews who were taken from their homes along that canal during WWII, pass by a buzzing flea market, chocolate shops, bakeries, and a specialty juggling shop…quite a way to go to work.

Immediately after the show, we are given the frightening news that a car has plowed into a group of people at nearby Central Station, the main hub of all the trains and metros not far away from us, resulting in the shutting down of all rail services. There is an immediate flurry of people checking on the safety of their visiting loved ones, as fears of terrorism flash through everyone's heads, given the recent vehicle attacks in Stockholm, Nice, Berlin, and London. But it turns out to be an accident. However, we discover that Roberta's partner Lianne was actually there, about 20 feet away, and witnessed the whole thing. As a result of this incident, traffic in the area has gotten jammed up, so our host-producer, Ellen, invites us all to the Theater's café for a drink while we wait for her to arrange taxis for us. A number of us continue our socializing back at the hotel bar, as we say goodbye to our good friend, Senior Tour Manager, and staunch supporter Jeremy Adams who has to fly back to New York to be at work at the Public in the morning. We've all signed a special *'Gabriels'* cutting board for him as a parting present. Tomorrow we finish our tour, and it brings up a lot of feelings in the company. We wish it could go on. Our work together in these plays has become steadily richer and richer, and the need they obviously fill for our audiences everywhere is palpable; our mission still feels fresh.

Marathon 3: Sunday, June 11

By the end of today we will have played a total of 214 performances in eight different venues across the world. As the shouting has escalated back in our country, the Gabriels have continued to talk and listen, refusing to give up on each other or the possibilities ahead.

The common fear of all final performances is that they will become primarily about that—tears welling up and overflowing—and given the nature of the last 14 months, the danger is understandable. But the six of us *'go to the cliff, hold hands, and jump,'* continuing to keep things vulnerable and alive without falling into the trap of sentiment. Our work continues right through our final day. It is a true celebration of everything we have worked for and learned together.

Standing backstage during the first show, listening lovingly to each scene for the final time, my reverie is broken by the sound of a man in the audience who gets up and makes his way noisily down from his seat into the backstage area, stops near me and grumbles in heavily-accented English, seemingly for my consumption, *'Thees…ees bullsheet.'* His apparent date catches up to him, and they push their way out. I smile wide at our associate stage manager, Jared Oberholtzer, who is standing nearby, looking as amused as I am. Keepin' it real.

During our dinner break between the last two plays. Holland Festival Artistic Director, Ruth Mackenzie, shows up to officially welcome us and say how excited she is to finally be completing her Gabriel Trilogy viewing. We first met her when she flew in to New York back in September for our opening night of **What Did You Expect?** and expressed her excitement about having us come to Holland. She then made it over to Brighton to see **Hungry**, and tonight she will finally finish the ride with us at our final performance of **Women of a Certain Age**.

Maryann enlists us all to do a special video shot she has imagined where she sweeps slowly across the empty set, then back over it to find all of us scattered across it, and one last time to, once again, an empty Gabriel kitchen. Ruth asks if she can also be a part of it and is, of course, welcomed in. The resulting shot is a beautifully bittersweet expression of the loss we are all feeling.

Our final performance of **Women of a Certain Age** is even more spontaneous than the first two and still wonderfully free of sentimentality, as we surprise ourselves with the ebb and flow of fresh discoveries, and move more and more freely through our lives together around the kitchen table, all overheard by a full house of welcome-but-unacknowledged neighbors. They have shown their enthusiasm at each of our earlier bows that day, but the surge of love and appreciation we feel at the final call will long be remembered by us all.

As we are called back to take yet another set of bows, Ruth steps out onto the stage among us and speaks forcefully to the audience about the momentous nature of this night, marking not only the end of our run at the festival but also of our entire tour and the whole arc of this project, which began at the Public Theater a year and a half ago. She lovingly insists that Richard join us onstage (a rare occurrence) and then, name by name, proceeds to call out every single member of our backstage team—stage management, sound, lighting, tour manager, everyone—to share in the glow of the moment. The inclusiveness is perfect and appreciated. Festival reps hand a colorful wooden Amsterdam tulip and present to each of us, as the applause continues, and we all stand together, taking in how far we've come.

Ruth gracefully thanks us on behalf of not only the audience today, but all of the audiences *'who have had the good fortune to get to witness this extraordinarily powerful and transformative work.'* It is an eloquent send-off for a rare and important accomplishment. This is what we do it for.

Afterwards, in the theater's café, we toast the tour with our Holland crew and producers, and then Richard talks to us. He is very proud of what we have accomplished together, right through this very last performance, never losing our focus, our aliveness. He says he spoke with Thomas Gabriel (the deceased playright character in the trilogy) last night and asked him about his statement that *'religion and theater are like this'* (the fingers of both hands intertwined).

'Religion,' he said, '—and I'm not talking about organized religion and all that, but religion in the purest sense—is the pursuit, I think, of how we can be good. And theater (for us) is the pursuit of art, of beauty. And together, those two elements are what we aspire to that give our lives meaning. And that's exactly what we have done. Goodness and beauty. It's not about how much money we can make or tickets we can sell. It's about taking goodness and beauty out into the world, and what effect we can have, and I think we've seen it in place after place, country after country, culture after culture. We have brought them something they hadn't seen before but recognized themselves in it. And not through shouting and divisiveness but simply conversation. We've done a good thing, an important thing, and I think we should be very proud of ourselves.'

All very casually, without conflict, without raising their voice, without drama. And yet, you are glued to their lips. The Holland Festival has obtained a hidden treasure from the States. The Gabriels is about us, as much as our own stories more than a hundred years old, like comparable European masterpieces by Anton Tsjechov or Henrik Ibsen or Strindberg. Because not only are they about the abyss itself, but, even closer to us, the way we stay deeply hidden deep from each other.

Wiibrand Schaan—*Cultuurpers*

The Gabriels feel like gusts of grief that got stuck in rooms in this noisy and confusing year...As in Chekhov. Who can presently be heard chuckling.

Loek Zonneveid—*De Gorene Amsterdammer*

Collected Tour Posters on the Gabriels set in Amsterdam—*left to right*: Shelly Vance, Heather Fichthorn, Theresa Flanagan, Maryann Plunkett (kneeling), Laura Brauner, Amy Warren, Jared Oberholtzer, Jay O. Sanders, Meg Gibson, Lynn Hawley, Jeremy Adams, Roberta Maxwell, Richard Nelson   photo: Jeff Harris

Celebrating the tour on the canals of Amsterdam—*left to right around the boat*: Shelly Vance, Theresa Flanagan, Cary Donaldson, Meg Gibson, Jared Oberholtzer, Jeff Harris, Amy Chen, Jay O. Sanders, Lynn Hawley, Roberta Maxwell, Lianne Ritchie, Cindy Nelson, Richard Nelson, Will Pickens, Laura Brauner, Maryann Plunkett

photo: our boat captain

The Gabriels, Election Year in the Life of One Family

Playwright/Director	**Richard Nelson**
Karin Gabriel	**Meg Gibson**
Hannah Gabriel	**Lynn Hawley**
Patricia Gabriel	**Roberta Maxwell**
George Gabriel	**Jay O. Sanders**
Mary Gabriel	**Maryann Plunkett**
Joyce Gabriel	**Amy Warren**
Scenic Designers	**Susan Hilferty and Jason Ardizzone-West**
Costume Designer	**Susan Hilferty**
Lighting Designer	**Jennifer Tipton**
Sound Designers	**Scott Lehrer and Will Pickens**
Properties Designer	**Claire M. Kavanah**
Production Stage Manager	**Theresa Flanagan**
Stage Manager	**Jared Oberholtzer**
Tour Manager	**Rebecca Sherman**
Assistant Tour Manager	**Heather Fichthorn**
Tour Production Manager	**Jeff Harris**
Tour Sound Designer	**Will Pickens**
Assistant Director	**Sash Bischoff**
Associate Costume Designer	**Mark Koss**
Assistant Lighting Designer	**Caitlin Smith-Rapoport**
Tour Audio Designer	**Laura Brauner**
Tour Props/Wardrobe Master	**Shelly Vance**

Production by the Public Theater, New York

Artistic Director	**Oskar Eustis**
Executive Director	**Patrick Willingham**
Production Executive	**Ruth Sternberg**
General Manager	**Jeremy Adams**
Tour Press and Marketing	**Candi Adams and Jared Fine**

Our production crew behind Kampnagel in Hamburg—*left to right*: Will Pickens, Rebecca Sherman, Laura Brauner, Jared Oberholtzer, Theresa Flanagan, Heather Fichthorn, Shelly Vance

photo: Lynn Hawley

The Apple Family

David Eden (Executive Tour Producer) and Jon DeVries in Brighton   photo: Sally Murphy

Maryann Plunkett and Jay O. Sanders in Brighton   photo: Pam Salling

Richard Nelson, Maggie Swing (Stage Manager), Maryann Plunkett, Pam Salling (Production Stage Manager), Mariann Mayberry, Sally Murphy, and Jesse Pennington in Berlin   photo: JOS

Mariann Mayberry and Sally Murphy in Vienna   photo: JOS

> **THE PUBLIC THEATER ANNOUNCES RICHARD NELSON'S AWARD-WINNING APPLE FAMILY PLAYS TO LAUNCH EUROPEAN TOUR**
>
> **APRIL 23–MAY 23, 2015**
>
> March 12, 2015 – The Public Theater (Artistic Director, Oskar Eustis; Executive Director, Patrick Willingham) announced today that Richard Nelson's award-winning ***THE APPLE FAMILY PLAYS: SCENES FROM LIFE IN THE COUNTRY*** will tour Europe for five weeks beginning April 23 at The Find Festival in Berlin. The other tour venues include The May International Festival in Weisbaden, Germany; The Brighton Festival in the United Kingdom; and the Vienna Festival in Austria where the tour will conclude on May 23. The tour is being produced by **David Eden, Executive Producer for David Eden Productions,** and co-produced and general managed by **Tim Smith for Pemberley Productions.**
>
> The European tour will feature original company members **Maryann Plunkett** (Barbara), **Jay O. Sanders** (Richard), **Jon DeVries** (Benjamin), and **Sally Murphy** (Jane), along with new cast members **Mariann Mayberry** (Marian) and **Jesse Pennington** (Tim).

2015 European Tour

THIS BOOK began as a project to document and share the experiences and lessons from the 2017 Gabriel Family World Tour, but its origins were the response to my Facebook postings during our original touring venture—with the Apples in Spring, 2015. That European tour, produced by David Eden and Tim Smith, was the first international introduction of the work we'd been exploring and evolving together from 2010–2013 at the Public Theater, commissioned and produced by Oskar Eustis and ultimately filmed by WNET for their *Theater Close-Up* program. We introduced a deceptively-simple, conversational style which, in fact, was a complex collaboration of actors, designers, and of course, writer/director, in search of a fresh aesthetic for our times. It was the embodiment of a philosophy celebrating the essential role of live theater and the centrality of the actor, opting for humanism rather than ideology; a bold experiment.

As Richard explained in an interview:

> "…In times like our own when human voices seem more disembodied than ever, when words seem pulled from their meanings and turned into rants and weapons, the theater can, I believe, be a necessary home for human talk. That is, a place where human beings talk about their worries, confusions, fears, and loves, and where they also listen."

Our appearances inspired numerous festival producers to immediately ask for more of Richard's work, resulting in The Gabriels. So, with an eye to thoroughness, I thought it appropriate to include those original posts here at the end, along with images from along the way.

Jesse Penningtion and Sally Murphy in Wiesbaden

Richard Nelson and Maryann Plunkett at Schaubühne in Berlin

all photos this page: JOS

Maryann Plunkett on Brighton Pier

Will Pickens (Sound Co-Designer/Live Mixer), Pam Salling, Tim Smith (Co-Producer/General Manager), Marie Yokoyama (Lighting Supervisor), and Maggie Swing in Vienna

A WORLD IN COMMON *an actor's diary*

Jon DeVries at the Schaubühne's café photo: JOS

Berlin, Germany

April 27, 2015

WE STARTED at noon. Or meant to. Our first full marathon began with some technical problem with the supertitles system, so we were held as they tried to resolve the issue. Twenty minutes or so later, and many worried, flashing looks on all sides—is this really how we're starting?—an announcement was made—first to us, then the audience—that at least this first play, *That Hopey Changey Thing*, would be translation-free. And so we began…hoping that the overall level of English comprehension would be sufficient to keep them with us. Turns out, it was. Very engaged and responsive audience. Perhaps it heightened everyone's attention, knowing that there would be no overhead assistance, perhaps we had a lot of English speakers in the house (I heard later that there was a group of overseas NYU students among them), but whatever it was, we were off and running. By the second play, *Sweet and Sad*, our supertitles were back, and the audience was settled in with us for the ride. The curtain calls were all very appreciative but a bit less vocal than our others, earlier in the week, had been, as though they all understood that today these were now four acts of a much larger play, rather than four separate entities. They leaned forward and listened closely to our conversations, becoming wordless guests at our table, as the Apple plays invite. As the day progressed, our audience swelled and became a breathing character of its own, so alive that we could feel their delight, discomfort, laughter, and tears at every twist and turn. Our third play, *Sorry*, came after a dinner break, and we all picked up easily together like old friends…they had become part of the family. Together, we were experiencing loss and revelations, questions, doubts, and dreams, as we faced down our shared fears about our world within the safe haven of a family that has learned to talk to each other, where anything can be questioned without judgement or penalty. Tears and laughter were flowing freely, every hurt countered by generous observations and stories to keep us afloat. **Regular Singing**, our fourth play, was the one Richard had reworked, trimming seven pages and restaging it in ways that have greatly improved its clarity and flow. It sang as it never had before, through every twist and turn we breathed together and heard every story for the first time. As the piece ended with Richard's beautiful coup de theatre of us turning out, addressing and acknowledging the audience, the faces we saw all around us were remarkably unguarded and present. The applause was passionate and they all rose to their feet—a far less common thing here than we see at home. We did four calls, I think. (We were all in a bit of a daze by then.) But it wasn't the applause or the bravos that were so affecting, it was the faces, the grateful sense of family, of speaking across all barriers, sharing concern for what it means to be human, to be alive at this time on our planet. And the reminder that we are all struggling, all doubting, all questioning. All yearning to find somewhere safe to talk and listen. Thank you, Richard Nelson. Thank you, all who took the ride. An unforgettable day. Now, on to Brighton!

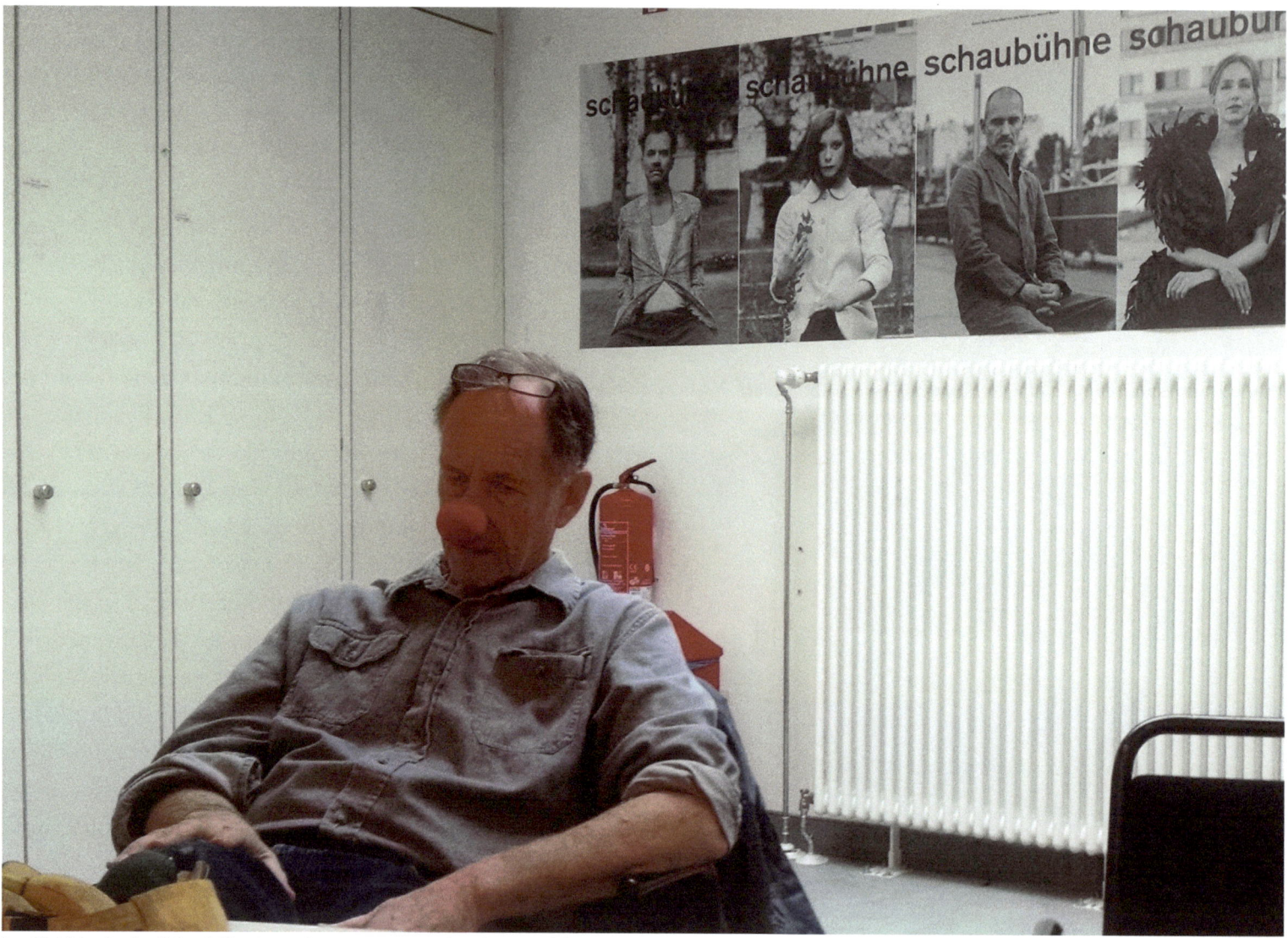

Jon DeVries in the Schaubühne's conference room under photos of the resident company

photo: JOS

Brighton, UK

May 5, 2015

Jay O. Sanders and Richard Nelson in the theater in Brighton   photo: Maryann Plunkett

AFTER TECHING all four plays in one day and no time for dress rehearsals, the Apple family opened the Brighton Festival over the weekend. The levels of trust we experienced onstage together were as focused and exhilarating as anything I can remember. We had worked such long hours and weeks to get to this point with two new cast members integrating themselves into our family, and Berlin had been a high watermark for our work, but we had continued to work, digging deeper and deeper into the details and rhythms of these delicately complex pieces, exploring the counterpoint of what we say to the central underlying concerns of the plays. Rumors of critics from London in the house, of course, only added to the mood. Always reminding ourselves to talk and listen. Ask real questions. No pronouncements. We are searching, we are lost. The need to talk. The need for family. Our first show for an English audience, *That Hopey Changey Thing*, went very well, despite still playing with the right levels for the mikes over the stage to keep us heard but the audience leaning in—a central philosophy and dynamic for these plays. The response afterwards was solid, but nothing like the enthusiasm we had just experienced in Berlin. But we were doing two shows that evening, so perhaps they were reserving their response for the end. But the second, *Sweet and Sad*, seemed to be jinxed. We experienced more technical problems in that one show than I think we've had in all of our previous performances over the last four years combined! Cue lights, sound levels, food issues, stage lighting miscues, backstage hand-offs, and actors running into walls as they exited, a couple of improvised mini-scenes to cover when actors were late for entrances due to miscommunications, and, as if all that wasn't enough, four prominently seated audience members in the front row on one side arrived inebriated and had fallen asleep before the play had even begun. But we stayed together and continued. At the curtain call, we were all amazed to hear enthusiastic cheers and see how moved the audience was. Richard came back excited and told us it was a beautiful performance. So, we regrouped with all departments to attend to the various issues and pressed on to Sunday. *Sorry* and *Regular Singing*. We had a voluntary rehearsal in the afternoon, that we all welcomed, to warm up together. Richard was being interviewed in a separate space that afternoon by Michael Billington, one of the most respected critics in England who writes for The Guardian and is known to be particularly tough. So, now we all knew he was out there. I imagine we all felt a bit vulnerable about his having been there the night before, but no one (that I heard, at least) said anything, and we just kept going. That night's performance of Sorry was a revelation—as connected, unpushed, fresh, and fully present—including the audience (our drunken friends were nowhere to be seen)—as I have ever experienced in the theater. Time, literally seemed to stand still. Whatever we said or did was answered *with* the united breath of everyone in that space and a shared desire to be nowhere but there, together, considering these questions, these observations, these lives. I was in awe of how joyous, empathetic, and free of judgement the room was. We all wanted to have this conversation. And we did. Mariann Mayberry, our very newest member who had joined us very late in the process with a nearly impossible amount of time, literally making our tour possible, positively glowed. It was a feeling like no other. And *Regular Singing* kept it going. Rising and falling through Richard Nelson's elegant, yet everyday, reflections of family, and how and why we live. We were again reminded that the English audiences are more reserved, so we tempered our expectations. But once the applause began, more than half of the audience came up out of their seats, rising to their feet and cheering. We had landed. On Monday, our second-ever marathon day continued the magic, opening with the best performance we have ever done of *Hopey* and the energy didn't waver as the day continued. At our dinner break, many of us were approached by audience members who saw us out and about and were eager to talk about how moved and involved they were—they couldn't wait to get back to their seats, to our table, for more. And we could feel it. Even as the theater got warmer than we would have liked, no one seemed to care. The hum of the day, the event, was palpable. And this time, our reserved English friends were all on their feet at once and loudly called us back to the stage for another call. Our producer, David Eden, a sweet, gentle man who adores these plays and our company, came down for a toast of Russian vodka he had brought and delivered the news that Michael Billington had written a rare five star review. A golden validation of everything we've been building. And the perfect capper for a well-deserved week off before Wiesbaden.

Brighton Apple Family poster

photo: JOS

Wiesbaden rehearsal from monitor on sound and stage management table *photo: JOS*

Wiesbaden, Germany

May 17, 2015

IN THE midst of a triumphant tour, Wiesbaden—home to one of the largest, most ornate theaters in the world which employs 600 people and presents 900 subsidized performances a year, land of thermal springs and spas and wealthy summer homes, a city left largely intact during WWII by the Allies who planned to use it as the center for their Western Bridge occupation force—Wiesbaden...dropped the ball.

The Apples are the first-ever American theater troupe invited to play at this festival (one of the oldest in Europe) and they decided to put us in a former slaughterhouse—Schlachthof—out of town, over by the train tracks, which had been turned into a rock and roll venue back in the 70s. We were told their idea was to attract a younger audience and possibly Americans from the various army bases in the area...but they fell short of their promise. Far short. To say these were the smallest audiences we have ever played to wouldn't do justice to the truth. Among the obstacles, we were in a remote, untested venue, performing on the weekend of the Feast of the Ascension, so many locals were out of town. On our first night, in a specially-constructed theater, designed to hold over 200 people, we had maybe 50, of whom fully a third were local officials and the theater directors there to welcome us on behalf of their town. After many translated speeches, congratulations, toasts, and honored-to-have-you-heres at our catered champagne reception, we were left to perform at our remote location to near-empty houses, including our third full marathon. However, the shows just continued to grow. We were so relaxed and focused and playing together for ourselves, that we discovered new depths and details, rediscovering these plays together. Those who were there—including a couple of welcome old friends from NY who now live in this part of the world—were extremely engaged, moved, and appreciative, and they saw top-level performances of these shows we've been exploring for so long. While one friend, the wonderful Steppenwolf actress, Rondi Reed—who had flown over specifically to join us for the last legs of our tour mixed with a personal vacation—slipped on her way out of a restaurant, seriously breaking her ankle in several places and has been in the hospital here, unable to attend any of our shows. (We are planning to visit her in the hospital today. Sally and Mariann have been over there regularly since it happened.) Perhaps an omen. By the final two shows yesterday, a few of our highest-ranking host producers from the Staatstheater returned to catch the second half of our four-play cycle, having seen the first two that celebratory first night, and were properly mortified. Afterwards, a couple of them went so far as to say they felt ashamed and deeply embarrassed on behalf of their festival and their town about their failure to deliver an audience, while a couple of others—notably a few drinks into their discomfort—laughed nervously as they tried to make light of what had happened. Given all the care and hours we had put in, our company was far from amused.

This stop will clearly be remembered by us all as the unforeseen pothole in an otherwise magical roadtrip. But we've already been assured—and reassured—that Vienna, one of the most beautiful cities in the world—our final stop and famously one of the most respected and well-run festivals in Europe—is already sold out! We're all hoping for a finale worthy of the amazing reception we felt so strongly in both Berlin and Brighton, and the love and artistry these plays have come to represent to us as a company. Today we rest, tomorrow we fly.

(Austrian TV has already promoted us in a special segment on one of their top arts shows, having sent a crew to Brighton to film all day at our four-play tech rehearsal:)

Reality-Show: "Apple Family Plays" / Kulturmontag vom 11.05.2015 um 23.10 Uhr

Tony-Preisträger Richard Nelson hat mit dem Stück "Apple Family Plays" eine intelektuelle Reality-Show geschaffen, die ab 19. Mai bei den Wiener Festwochen…

TVTHEK.ORF.AT

Tim Smith and Pam Salling herd the actors

Jesse Pennington, Sally Murphy and Mariann Mayberry

photos: JOS

Vienna, Austria

May 24, 2015

WE PLAYED them one by one. For the first time on this tour, we had the luxury of teching, reviewing, then playing a single show each day, as the Apples helped kick off the 65th season of the Vienna Festival. *'Toto, we're not in Wiesbaden any more!'* Set in a theater within a central complex of major museums (the Museumsquartier Wien), we were met with a level of support, professionalism, curiosity, and promotion that was like arriving on another planet. Not to mention, the audiences—every show was PACKED! People listened and read supertitles, responding audibly enough to constantly remind us they were with us, but never attempting to make us into a sitcom. They understood they were welcomed into our dining room but not being played to, as is the style of these pieces. We could feel their presence every step, but the six of us talked and listened solely to each other. Over those first four nights, the plays blossomed freshly, finding a new ease and resonance. Our two new cast members, Mariann Mayberry and Jesse Pennington, both found an exciting new level of confidence and clarity which helped lift us all to new heights. Our familiarity (the perfect word) allowed us to ride long waves of overlaps and interjections together without obscuring what the audience needed to hear. Long speeches, interrupted by side conversations, questions, and observations, rose effortlessly to the surface of what could easily have been unlistenable chaos, and instead simply sounded like how we talk to each other. The joy of this accomplished, well-oiled company of actors playing these extraordinary scripts together over several years—I would have to say—in my forty years of professional experience—it simply

Exterior of our Vienna Theater   photo: JOS

The Apples in performance (*clockwise from left*): Mariann Mayberry, Jon DeVries, Sally Murphy, Jesse Pennington, Jay O. Sanders, Maryann Plunkett   photo: Joan Marcus

Inside our Vienna Theater   photo: JOS

doesn't get any better than this. One of the most unique elements, of course, is the length of time over which we have been able to grow together and with Richard. Sadly, opportunities like this are very rare. Over the course of the last five years, in our own lives, we have each experienced personal loss—parents, siblings, in-laws, our own life-threatening illnesses—and all had this second family from which to draw strength and support, as we continued to come back together to give birth to, then rediscover, these plays.

The week grew with the plays, as our audience stepped further and further into Rhinebeck and the lives of the Apples. The quality of their listening noticeably deepened. After the introduction to our family's world in **That Hopey Changey Thing**, they returned to our house in Rhinebeck for what felt more and more like solace—a place where they could listen to vulnerable conversations between imperfect people, like themselves, who were trying to navigate their uncertain lives and make sense of their place in the world. What could be more universal? And, on top of that, they have their own elections coming up—just as the UK did the week after we played in Brighton. And everyone relating their own disillusionment and frustration with their political landscapes and the direction of our world to those of the Apples. Their laughter, tears, and overflow sounds spoke of people sitting with us at our table, considering their own lives, not looking to be entertained. We were at home together.

The responses after each show were very strong, and especially at the end of four, as clearly many of them had been with us all week. They brought us back to the stage many times and applauded vigorously, becoming more and more vocal, as the week progressed. But the communion was much more than the applause. What we saw were the open, smiling, deeply-moved faces looking back at us, nodding repeatedly and lighting up when we met their eyes. This was personal.

Our final marathon. We are all a bit in denial that this is ending. It's hard to believe that these plays, which still have so much life and power in them, will not be seen further in New York (which has not had an extended run, nor ever seen this marathon) —or in London. But so goes the ephemeral nature of the theater.

We experienced together a full day of the larger four-act *'play'* of this cycle with the most relaxed, open, sharp and quickly-thought freshness of our whole tour—the perfect farewell run. We all agreed that the work of Jon DeVries as Uncle Benjamin was particularly inspired. The world he has created and inhabited for himself, playing an accomplished actor with an ever-diminishing memory, has knocked us all out—heartbreakingly alive as he continued to search for clues in a mysteriously fading world. Sally Murphy's Jane lit up story after story, finding countless new facets to everything from her research on American manners to her hysterical rendition of the origins of *George Washington Crossing the Delaware*, and relating the country's broken party system to two divorcing parents. Jesse Pennington brought a unique quirkiness to Tim, charting a complex journey from outsider to embedded presence, seriously cracking me up with his Rhinebeck Aerodrome speech, and surprising us all with his warm singing voice. Mariann Mayberry—our company hero—sailed through as though she'd always been with us. Her humor and playfulness, intelligence and heart, fearlessness and hard, hard work were truly unbelievable and literally made our tour possible. I'm only sorry she was denied the time to find her feet early enough in this process to have been able to enjoy this run as much as she said she finally began to on this—our final—day.

And Maryann Plunkett—'*What would we do without Barbara?*' I will confess to being less than impartial, but these plays revolve around her. Her heart, her ever-attentive touch, the deep wells of her eyes. She lives and breathes these plays. "*In Barbara's house I shall dwell, for long as days shall be.*' The performances she has given over the last five years...don't feel like performances. As her husband and best friend, I can simply say, I have been privileged to have lived these plays with her.

Which comes to me. Richard Apple. I stayed simple, despite my well-known love of theatricality. I stayed honest and vulnerable, conversational and unsure, questing for active thought—our '*willed amnesia*'—remembering lines as they came out. And each night, I did my best to make my way forward step by step, through the questions at hand. That was my task. I've learned a lot about trusting my simplest self and am very grateful that Richard asked me to join this family.

Our marathon day flew by, gracefully. We made every twist and turn together, and the audience breathed and leaned with us as we went. There was one moment in **Sweet and Sad** when Barbara notes an entry in a found diary 'September 11, Breakfast, WOW' she reads. 'WOW?' we ask. '*We figured it meant Windows on the World.*' There was an audible gasp from one particular person in the audience that was so personal and went on for a few beats, and it shot straight through us. We hadn't heard a reaction like that since New York. A number of us became very emotional, as that memory resonated with us. A breath, and we went on. The day was a glorious ending for our tour.

At the final curtain call, the whole packed house jumped directly to their feet and cheered and clapped in rhythm calling us back many times. But again, it was their faces—their eyes, their grateful smiles, their familiar nods. They knew us, recognized us. And somehow, they knew we knew them, too.

And so we live. Sometimes we come together. Something brings us together. And some days we are alone. But it's those days together that remind us, why we live. Or, maybe it's—how. How—we live...(Lights fade.)

END OF PLAY

The Apples celebrate with our new friend and fairy godmother, Mariam Younes *(third from the front left, just over Maryann's head)* at her uncle's restaurant in Berlin   photo: the waiter

Jay O. Sanders

In Memoriam

Mariann Mayberry (1965–2017)

MARIANN WAS our angel. She quite literally saved our Apple Family tour, stepping in very last minute to learn four complicated, interwoven plays. Fed by her spirit, our pride in our years of hard work together, and a shared love of these plays, we rehearsed every possible moment of every day. And in the end, we triumphed, her bravery having made it all possible. After Vienna, a group of us drove down through the Swiss Alps to celebrate in and around Venice for a week, before putting her on a plane back to Chicago to begin rehearsals for yet another play. We all knew she was battling cancer, but she was very private, and it was impossible to know how much it had taken hold. Nor did she—but she continued, nonstop, clearly welcoming every distraction, joyously sharing her talent and life-force right to the end. We thank you, love you, and miss you, MM.

Mariann onstage at the Schaubühne
photo: Maryann Plunkett

Mariann with Jon Devries

(left to right) Maryann Plunkett, Jay O. Sanders, Sally Murphy, Mariann, and Maggie Swing in Venice   *photo: the waiter*

www.ingramcontent.com/pod-product-compliance
Lightning Source LLC
Chambersburg PA
CBHW041322290426

44108CB00004B/102